The Self-Sufficient Backyard: A Complete Guide to Start Your Own Sustainable Backyard Mini Farm

Kickstart Your Homestead Garden And Produce All the Food You Need Off the Grid

Ben Rinner

indirect, that are incurred as a result of the use of the information contained within this document, including, but not limited to, errors, omissions, or inaccuracies.

Table of Contents

Introduction:

The Beauty of Backyard Farming

Have you ever stared at your flower garden and wondered, "What more can I do? Can I grow fruits, vegetables, maybe even start a mini farm?"

These days, more and more people are getting interested in backyard farming. There is a distinct kind of comfort and reassurance that comes from knowing that you have a self-sufficient mini farm in your backyard (or front yard). No matter how high the prices of food go in the market, you won't be worried because you will have your own fresh fruits, vegetables, and maybe even livestock right outside your house.

Over time, you might even be able to make a profit out of your mini farm.

Not only will you save and potentially make money off your mini farm, you will have the option to grow any kind of food you want and you will always get the assurance of high-quality food.

But if you have never tried backyard farming, it may sound like an overwhelming endeavor. The mere thought of starting a mini farm can already make your head spin!

The good news is, you have this book to give you some tips and guidance along the way.

Starting and maintaining your own mini farm is a lifelong learning process, but even if you have no experience, you can still learn how to become an off-grid farmer.

In this book, you will learn all of the fundamental information you need to start your own small farm in your backyard. All of the chapters in this book will help you understand what benefits you can get from growing your own food, what is involved in backyard farming, and how to get started. You will also learn about the different elements of a mini farm to help you determine what will work for you.

By the end of this book, you will feel more confident and excited about the journey. You will also have the knowledge you need to create a plan for how you will start creating your mini farm. With this knowledge, starting and maintaining a mini farm in your backyard will be more doable for you.

You will even learn a few tips and tricks for how to make money through your mini farm. There is much to learn throughout this book and you can even visit https://selfreliantbooks.com for more incredible information about self-sufficiency and homesteading. If you're ready to discover the fundamentals of backyard farming, turn the page, and let's begin!

Chapter 1:

All About Starting Your Own

Backyard Mini Farm

Backyard farming is all about using your land to grow your own fruits, vegetables, herbs, and spices. If you have enough space, you can also raise animals like livestock, beneficial insects, and even fish! To do this, you need to know how to plan, prepare, and take the necessary steps to transform your ordinary backyard into a mini farm.

The Benefits of Having a Mini Farm in Your Backyard

Transforming your backyard into a mini farm takes a lot of time and effort. But the process of doing so can be extremely enjoyable and fulfilling. And the best part is, this endeavor offers tons of benefits to your life. Let's go through some of the best advantages of having a mini farm in your backyard.

It's Easy to Start a Mini Farm... Even if You're a Beginner

One of the first benefits of backyard farming is its manageability. With the right knowledge and an organized plan, you can easily start your mini farm. Since the farm will be a small one, you can start and maintain it on your own. You won't have to spend money on the salaries of workers who will plant, care for, or harvest your crops. Even if you plan to raise animals on your mini farm, you can do this by yourself.

Even if you are a beginner, you can create a plan for your mini farm using everything you will learn from this book. And if you discover that something doesn't work in your mini farm—like if you notice that your plants aren't thriving in a certain location—you can make the decision to improve the situation. Over time, you will learn how to tend to your plants and raise your animals well. Starting and maintaining a mini farm is a process where you will learn new things. This, in turn, will allow you to make your mini farm sustainable in the long run.

You Don't Have to Spend a Lot to Start Your Mini Farm

While some hobbies might cause you to spend a lot just to start, backyard farming is different. Seeds, gardening tools, and other things you will need for your backyard farm are fairly inexpensive. You can start with simple plants and use what you already have in your garden. And, later, if you are able to make money from your mini farm, you can also start thinking about investing in more expensive equipment and tools that will make your mini farm even more profitable.

You Can Customize Your Mini Farm

Another excellent benefit of mini farming is the customization it allows. Since you will be building a small farm in your backyard, you can choose which fruits, veggies, spices, or herbs to grow, what growing methods to use, and how to arrange your plants in the garden. If you also want to beautify your home, you can learn how to create edible landscapes. And when your plants flourish, they will instantly transform your plain old backyard into a stunning garden where you can harvest fresh produce. Plus, each time you eat the food from your garden, you will have the assurance that it doesn't contain any pesticides or chemicals.

You can also decide when to start raising animals, which animals to raise, and where to house them. You have so many options in terms of the types of animals to raise on your farm, and your choices will depend on your aim for raising animals, the space you have in your garden, and whether or not you think you can care for certain animals. Once you have gotten the hang of maintaining your mini farm, you can also decide whether you will turn this into a small business and make money out of it.

You Can Grow Plants Indoors for Your Mini Farm

Your mini farm doesn't have to end in your backyard either. If you choose to grow your plants in containers, you can bring those containers inside your home. This is especially helpful during the winter seasons if you are growing plants that aren't tolerant of cold or windy conditions. Doing this will also allow you to grow more plants to fill your farm.

You'll Save Money

While you will be spending some money at the beginning to buy seeds, containers, gardening tools, and even simple equipment, in the long run, your mini farm will help you save a lot of money. Since you can harvest fresh produce in your garden or even have a constant supply of animal products, you will save a lot on food costs. And if you keep growing different kinds of plants or raising different kinds of animals, you can enjoy a wide variety of foods fresh from your garden.

You Will Improve Your Diet

When you know that you can harvest food directly from your backyard, you won't have to buy food products in supermarkets. This will be a big improvement in your diet since many food items today contain plenty of unnecessary ingredients. Growing your own food reduces your intake of processed foods, which will get you one step closer to a healthier lifestyle. Freshly-picked fruits and veggies also contain more vitamins and minerals compared to those that have undergone processing.

You Will Increase Your Physical Activity

Gardening is a physical activity and so is caring for animals. By taking up this hobby, you will increase your daily physical activity. It's common knowledge that regular exercise is essential for a healthy lifestyle. Therefore, the additional physical activity you will get from tending to your farm and raising different kinds of animals will make you healthier too. Pair this with the new diet of fresh fruits and vegetables you will be eating, and you will surely improve your overall health and well-being.

You Can Work on Your Farm to Relieve Stress

Gardening is also a great stress reliever. There is nothing like spending some quality time in nature. If you're feeling stressed, you can spend time on your mini farm, and the act of caring for your plants, feeding your animals, or just sitting in your garden while breathing fresh air will make you feel calmer. Setting aside time each day to do this will help you feel better no matter how stressful your life is.

You Will Become Self-Reliant

Having a sustainable mini farm will also make you self-reliant. You won't just learn how beautiful and beneficial nature is, but you will also come to appreciate the time it takes for a seed to grow into a plant that bears fruit. You will discover how much care and effort it takes to raise young animals into adults. And when it's time for you to reap the fruits of your labor, you will realize just how self-reliant you have become. This is one of the most important benefits of having a mini farm in your backyard.

You Can Teach Your Children About Farming and Healthy Food

While you can easily start and maintain a mini farm on your own, it doesn't have to be a solitary activity. You can also invite the rest of your family to join in. If you have children, invite them to join you while farming. Then you can take this as an opportunity to teach them all about how plants grow, the proper care of animals, and even the importance of healthy food. The activities done while maintaining a mini farm are very interesting to young children. Take advantage of that interest and use it to teach your child some important lessons that they will need in life.

You Can Even Boost the Economy of Your Locale

At some point, you might decide to make money from your farm. Once you have established your plants and animals, you can start making plans for how to make a living from what your farm produces. There are so many ways to do this. All you have to do is think about what you can offer to consumers and how to sustain those products. For instance, if you plan to sell vegetables, you have to make sure that you are growing continuous harvests. Or if you plan to sell fresh honey, you need to make sure that your beehives will produce this food constantly. It's all about careful planning and making an effort to keep your farm going.

You Will Help the Environment

Having your own mini farm will also make a positive impact on the environment. Instead of relying on the food industry, you will be relying on your own crops and livestock. Also, having a backyard garden is a great way to attract pollinators. These insects, in turn, will affect your neighbors as they will help pollinate plants from all over your neighborhood.

You Can Contribute to Your Community

If you can, encourage others in your community to start their own mini farm. Or at the very least, they should buy their fresh produce from you. When people in the community work together like this, it creates peace and harmony within the community itself. And if everyone starts growing their own food, everyone can even learn from each other. You will also have the option to trade produce with your neighbors. That way, you can enjoy a wide variety of food products without having to grow everything yourself!

Hunger is an issue all over the world. But we can avoid this if we all try to start our own mini farms. Although this is easier said than done, we will all benefit a lot if we don't always depend on huge farms. Now that you understand how beneficial mini farming truly is, you can feel more motivated to grow your own food instead of spending too much money just to put food on the table.

Things to Consider Before You Start

Knowing the benefits of having a mini farm in your backyard is just the beginning. Before you can start making a plan, you must first think about certain considerations. While it's true that you can customize your mini farm however you wish, you might encounter some limitations if you don't consider the following factors first.

Think About Your Reason for Starting a Mini Farm

First of all, you need to think about why you would like to start a mini farm in your backyard. Do you have too much free time and you just want to do something productive with it? Do you want to follow a healthier diet by only eating foods that you grow yourself? Or have you always been interested in farming and you now want to pursue that interest?

There is no right or wrong reason for wanting to start a mini farm. The important thing is to find out your own reason so that you can use it to keep yourself motivated when you encounter difficulties along the way.

Do Some Research

Once you know why you want to start a mini farm, the next step is to find out how you will do this. As an aspiring farmer, you have a lot to learn. Starting a mini farm isn't something you should take lightly. It involves a lot of steps and the more prepared you are, the easier your journey will be. When it comes to research, here are some tips for you:

- Try to get some hands-on experience. If you know anyone who owns a farm, volunteer to help out once in a while. As you do this, you can ask questions and even observe to gain the knowledge and skills you need when it's time for you to start your backyard farm.

- Visit different kinds of farms to learn more about how they work. For instance, visiting vegetable farms will help you learn all about growing these crops. Or visiting a local farm where they also raise livestock will give you an idea of what to expect when raising these kinds of animals.

- Visit some local farmers' markets too. That way, you will have a better idea of what is currently available, what people buy, and even some pricing information.

- If you plan to eventually turn your mini farm into a business, you can start doing market research as early as possible. This includes learning about your potential customers (the people who live in your community), distribution channels (where you can sell your products), the permits you need to start your business, and more.

- It would also be very helpful to speak to the other farmers in your community, as well as your potential customers, to give you an idea of what is lacking. This will give you an edge when you start selling products from your farm.

Doing research is a valuable way to learn more about farming. This is a very important step that will increase your chances of success in the long run.

Decide if You Will Farm as a Hobby or if You Want to Make a Profit

Next, think about whether you will have a mini farm to provide your family with a sustainable source of food or if you'll also want to expand and make a profit. Of course, if you choose the former, your journey will be much easier than if you choose the latter. You will also need more space if you plan to turn your mini farm into a business.

Prepare Yourself for the Physical Work

While the physical activity you will get from working on your mini farm is good for you, it's important to prepare yourself first. This is especially important if you have been living a sedentary lifestyle up until now. Owning a mini farm involves a lot of hard work. It's fulfilling and enjoyable, but the physical labor involved is not a small thing, especially at the beginning when you have to set everything up. If you would like to prepare yourself for the additional physical activity, consider adding light exercises to your daily routine to make you stronger and increase your endurance.

Consider What You Will Do if You Encounter Any Challenges

Whether you are about to start your mini farm from scratch or you are already growing some crops and you are just planning to expand, you will encounter some challenges along the way. This is where things will get difficult. But if you prepare for such challenges, you will be able to handle them more effectively. Don't worry because we will be discussing the possible mistakes and challenges you might encounter when starting and maintaining your backyard farm along with ways to avoid or overcome them.

Assess Your Land

You cannot start a mini farm without land. If you already have land (like a big backyard), good for you! Now, you have to assess it. Some things to look into while assessing your land include:

- You need to have a steady supply of water to nourish your plants and animals. If your land doesn't have this, you will have to think of how you will transport water from the closest water source to your farm.

- In line with the water supply, consider the price of this essential factor too. This will help you determine what types of plants you can grow and what types of animals you can raise.

- As important is the quality of your soil. If you have a big piece of land but it has poor soil, you won't be able to grow healthy plants. You can take a small sample of the soil on your land and have it tested. If your soil is rich and contains plenty of nutrients, you can start planting right away. But if you have poor soil, you would have to think of different ways to grow healthy plants such as growing them in pots or using organic fertilizer for nourishment. Most soil-testing labs will provide you with a report detailing which elements are lacking in your soil and which elements are excessive, and they can provide recommendations on how to amend your soil.

- If you plan to raise animals on your farm, think about the infrastructure and facilities you will need. For example, if you want to grow fish, you will need a pond. Or if you will take care of bees, you will need containers for the beehives. Of course, you should also have enough space on your land to raise these animals.

- Go around your community to check out the proximity of your farm to the local markets. This is essential if you plan to make a profit as it will help you discover where you can sell your products and whether or not your business idea is feasible.

It's also a good idea to think about your neighbors before setting up your land as a farm with plants, animals, or both. For instance, if you have neighbors that value peace and quiet, you might want to avoid raising animals that make a lot of noise. On the other hand, if you know that your neighbors only eat organic produce, you might want to focus on growing organic fruits and vegetables, and talk to your neighbors about it, as they can potentially turn into your regular customers.

Think About the Weather

Also, think about the weather in your locale. Different types of plants grow and thrive in different weather conditions. The same thing goes for animals. Do your research to find out which plants and animals will flourish on your farm and which ones might pose more of a challenge for you. In some cases, you might have to grow plants indoors if the weather outside isn't right for them.

If you don't have a piece of land yet, you should still consider all of these things before buying land. Think about the cost of the land versus the potential challenges you will have creating a mini farm on this particular piece of land.

By considering all of these factors, you will already have a better idea of what components you can include in your farm. From here, you can brainstorm the plans for your mini farm.

Chapter 2:

What Makes a Mini Farm?

Mini farms can include different elements. Growing fruits and vegetables is just one aspect of this beneficial undertaking. In this chapter, we will go through the different elements of a mini farm. This will help you understand what you can potentially include in your backyard farm. Of course, at the end of the day, the decision of what to include lies with you.

Plants

Plants are one of the main elements of a backyard farm. When it comes to plants, you can opt for fruits, vegetables, herbs, and spices. If you want to beautify your garden too, you can also plant flowers.

When growing plants on your mini farm, having a wide variety of crops will be beneficial for you. This will also make your mini farm more sustainable as you won't feel bored with harvesting and eating the same things over and over again. Even if you don't plant ornamental flowers in your backyard, you can still increase the aesthetic appeal by landscaping with edible plants. For instance, planting fruit trees will provide you with shade, flowers in the spring, and fruits too. You can also choose to plant edible flowers like nasturtiums or pansies that you can add to salads.

Animals

After you have established the crops on your mini farm, you can make the decision to raise animals too. The types of animals you can raise will depend on where you live, how much space you have, and your commitment to raising the type of animals you have chosen. For example, if you live in the suburbs or in the city, it's not ideal to raise big animals like horses or cows.

But even if you have limited space, there is still a wide range of animals you can raise such as chickens, rabbits, and quails. You can even consider raising fish or bees if you think you can care for them well. From learning how to purchase young animals to discovering what they need at each stage of growth, there is a lot for you to learn. Adding animals to your backyard mini farm will elevate your entire farming experience. Plus, taking care of animals is a lot of fun too!

Of course, raising animals in your backyard also means that you will have access to animal products like meat, eggs, milk, honey, and even wool from sheep. If you plan to make money from your mini farm, including this element will also be more profitable for you. Just remember that raising animals—no matter what kind—takes a lot of time and effort. You also need to have the willingness to learn all about raising the specific animal you have chosen until you can take advantage of the products they can give you.

Other Elements

Apart from plants and animals, there are other elements you can add to your mini farm too. These elements will make your backyard farm complete. These elements will also make your farming experience more enjoyable. If you want to make your mini farm a place where your family gathers and spends time together, one of the best things you can do is to include some outdoor cooking equipment. When you're living off the grid, cooking outside on your mini farm just makes sense!

Having an outdoor kitchen on your mini farm is very convenient. The most basic type of kitchen layout would cost you around $500.00. Of course, the actual price would depend on how simple or elaborate you want your kitchen to be. But just imagine harvesting your crops straight from your garden, adding them to your dishes, and cooking them outside right where you've harvested them. There are many options for you when it comes to cooking installations:

- **Brick oven**

    There are many ways for you to build a brick oven outside your home. If you love baking and you want to use the freshest ingredients for your baked dishes, having a brick oven is the best choice.

- **Outdoor grill**

  Having an outdoor grill in your backyard will allow you to create different kinds of grilled dishes without having to go back and forth from your kitchen to your farm. If you plan to grow herbs in your garden, place your grill close to those plants so that they are easily accessible to you.

- **Solar oven**

  As the name suggests, a solar oven works on solar power. As long as the sun is in the sky, you can use this oven to cook without having to consume electricity. Just plan the placement of the solar oven well so that you can make the most of the sun's energy whenever you need it.

- **Solar stove**

  A solar stove also uses solar energy to cook or heat your food. This is a sustainable option that's also environmentally friendly. As with a solar oven, think carefully about where you will place your solar stove. There are many types of solar stoves to choose from including box cookers, panel cookers, parabolic cookers, and tube cookers.

- **Wood-burning stove**

  If you live next to a forest or you have access to a lot of firewood, you may consider having a wood-burning stove on your mini farm. Modern wood-burning stoves reduce emissions, which means that they produce minimal to no smoke. This is another eco-friendly way to cook your food while staying warm when the weather is cold.

Of course, cooking isn't the only thing you can do on your mini farm. Apart from these cooking installations, you can also add other beneficial components like:

- A roof to keep you shaded when you need to rest.

- A sink so that you can always wash your hands or the ingredients you harvest from your farm.
- Storage spaces where you can store your cooking or gardening supplies.
- A mini refrigerator where you can place cold drinks for yourself and your guests.

Go back to the advantage of having the freedom to customize your mini farm. This includes all of the elements you will add to it. When making the plans for your mini farm, don't forget to include any other elements you want on it too.

Chapter 3:

Starting a Mini Farm in Your

Backyard

Now that you have learned the fundamentals of a backyard mini farm, it's time to learn how to start. To help you understand each aspect better, you will learn them individually. First, let's begin with growing plants.

The Best Beginner Tips to Start Your Mini Farm

Starting your own mini farm at home is a complex process, but it doesn't have to be difficult. The key here is to know what to expect, come up with a plan, and keep going even if you encounter some challenges along the way. To help you get started, here are some important tips.

Start Small

While there is nothing wrong with wanting to have a flourishing mini farm filled with plants, animals, and other elements, you can easily feel overwhelmed if you try to do too many things right away. To enjoy your farming experience, it's better to start small. Once you have your plan, start by choosing a few types of crops and plant those first. Doing this will give you a feel of what tending to a garden is all about. As you get used to farming and you see that your crops are thriving, you can expand your garden.

Make a commitment to spend at least half an hour in your garden each day. That would give you enough time to care for the few plants you have started growing. And when you start expanding your mini farm, make it a point to spend more time maintaining it too. By taking things slow, you will become more knowledgeable, motivated, and relaxed with this important endeavor.

Make the Most of Your Space

No matter what the size of your backyard is, there are many ways to maximize it. Start with the space that you have, then think of ways to grow as many plants and raise as many animals as you can without compromising any of them. If you have a small space, you can always opt for vertical gardening or using structures like cages, trellises, and the like to support your plants. The same thing goes if you decide to raise animals. The space you have available is a big factor that will help you determine what to include on your farm.

Decide What to Include on Your Farm

If one of your main reasons for starting a mini farm is to become self-reliant, then you should grow crops that you and your family like to eat. It wouldn't be enjoyable for you to grow fruits or veggies that nobody will eat after you harvest them. Make a list of all your favorite fruits, vegetables, herbs, and spices. Ask your family members too. Next, narrow down the list by eliminating any that aren't likely to thrive in your locale.

This can give you a rough idea of which plants you'd like to consider including on your mini farm. If this is your first time growing produce, you may want to start with plants that are easy to grow. This will keep you motivated, especially when you see that all of your efforts are giving you amazing results. You can skip ahead to chapters 5 and 6 for some recommendations on plants that are easy for beginners to get started with to give you more ideas for your list or help you narrow it down.

This is also the time when you can start thinking about what other elements to add to your mini farm. You can grow flowers, ornamental plants, or medicinal plants too. You can also begin to think about whether or not you will raise animals on your farm or add other elements like storage spaces or cooking installations. Having a plan makes it easier for you to do what you need for your farm. Of course, you can always make changes to your plan depending on the results of your initial efforts and the discoveries you make along the way.

Aim for Diversity

When deciding what to include in your mini farm, aim for variety. Growing the same plants means having the same kinds of produce on your table each time. This isn't ideal as you might get bored with your farm after some time. Also, you should know that plants grow at different rates. So if you want to have fresh produce all year round, you need a diverse selection of crops in your garden that can be harvested at different times.

Think About the Landscape

If you already have a plan for which plants to grow, you will be able to come up with a design for your landscape too. If you want to feel good about your mini farm, plan the landscape carefully. Consider the aesthetic appeal and the functionality of the layout. Also, you need to be strategic in terms of positioning your plants. Any plants that need a lot of sunlight should be in a spot where they will get enough sun. If you have plants that grow better with companion plants, position them next to other plants. In the following chapters, you'll learn some growing techniques and requirements for specific plants that can help you further plan your landscape design.

Learn About Composting

Composting is an essential part of growing plants in a mini farm. Since you will be growing a wide range of plants in a small space, those plants will demand a lot from your soil. While fertilizers can help make your plants healthier, composting ensures that the soil is rich with natural materials. You will also save a lot of money because you won't have to spend on fertilizers. Composting is a process that involves mixing various organic materials like leaves, food scraps, yard waste, and even animal products together. The resulting mixture (called compost) will be rich in beneficial organisms and plant nutrients to keep your crops healthy. If you can include this practice in your farming routine, it will be extremely beneficial for your plants.

To start composting, you will need a big bin on your mini farm. This is where you will dump all of the organic materials for your compost. After some time, you can scoop the compost and use it to fertilize your soil. Spreading a layer of compost over your crops will protect the soil underneath. This will also reduce the water requirements of your plants while preventing the growth of weeds. While the compost decomposes further, it will improve the quality of your soil. Just make sure that your compost bin has a lid so that it won't attract the local wildlife. This is especially important if you plan to add food scraps to your compost. You should also mix the materials often so that it will take less time for them to break down.

Determine if You Can Raise Animals Too

When you have established the garden in your mini farm, it's time to think about the possibility of raising animals too. As with plants, it's important to start small when raising animals. You should consider the space you have for these living things. It's not ideal to try and cram several animals in a small space. You shouldn't underestimate the space needed for growing animals. Even chickens, which are small animals, need chicken coops to live in. These animal homes require substantial space. And if you will raise several types of animals, make sure to plan their placements carefully first.

When it comes to raising animals, you should also research permit requirements, licenses, and the zoning ordinances of your locale. You don't want to spend a lot of money on the habitats of animals only to find out that you aren't allowed to raise the kind of animals you prepared for. No matter what type of animal you choose, make sure to do a lot of research first. Researching will also enable you to find the best and most reputable suppliers or breeders in your area.

Save Water by Using the Rain

You will need a lot of water for your farm. You need water to nourish your plants, clean your gardening tools, and for nourishing your animals too. If you plan to cook on your mini farm, you will also need water for that. Or if you plan to raise fish, you will need a lot of water for that too. Using this much water might cost a lot but if you use rainwater, you won't have to spend so much. To collect rainwater, place a big barrel or bin outside. You can even use large stock pots whenever it rains. Just make sure to use the water right away so it won't become a breeding ground for mosquitoes and other insects.

Allow Yourself to Learn While Farming

Maintaining a mini farm is a process. It's not something you make, then leave on its own. You need to continuously tend to your plants, care for your animals, and maintain the other elements on your farm. You should also allow yourself to continue learning while you are farming. For instance, if you had your heart set on a certain type of plant only to discover that it won't thrive in your garden, either find a new way to grow that plant (maybe in a container or in another part of your farm) or find other plants to grow.

Even while raising animals, you will learn so many new things! From being able to determine how healthy your animals are to finding out how to breed your animals and everything in between, you will discover so much. Even if you make mistakes along the way, don't beat yourself up about it. Always remember that this is a learning process that will make you a better farmer as time goes by.

Reassess Your Farm Regularly

It's also important to regularly check all the parts of your farm regularly. Doing this allows you to assess the health of your plants and animals, and the state of the other elements in your farm. Each time you evaluate the different aspects of your farm, you should also decide whether you need to make some changes. This is also the best time for you to determine if you can expand your mini farm by adding more elements to it.

No matter what your reason is for starting a mini farm, remember that it will entail a lot of work. But the work will be enjoyable and fulfilling, especially if you start seeing your efforts pay off in the form of bountiful plants, healthy animals, and functional elements.

Chapter 4:

All About Planting on Your Mini

Farm

If you want to have a sustainable mini farm in your backyard, you'll need to learn how to plant and care for different kinds of fruits, vegetables, herbs, and spices. Whether you have a big piece of land or a small one, planning the plants on your farm is of the essence. You have to think about the types of plants, the placements, and even the growing methods to use. Even if you are a beginner, you can successfully grow different kinds of plants from seeds to maturity... and you will start learning how in this chapter.

The Most Common Growing Methods to Use

By now, you should have already made your list of plants and narrowed it down to the ones that are feasible to grow in your area. Next, it will be time to decide on growing methods for the plants you have chosen and to plan the layout of your mini farm. Here are some ideas to get you started.

Companion Planting

This growing method is ideal if you would like to reduce the risk of pest infestations. You can also opt for this growing method when you don't have a lot of space on your farm. Companion planting involves planting specific types of plants next to each other for the reason that they will benefit each other. For instance, planting shade-loving crops next to tall ones that provide shade. Some examples of plants that would grow well next to tall crops are basil and lettuce. You can also plant fast-growing crops next to slow-growing ones so that you will always have fresh produce to harvest.

As for the reduction of pest infestation, you can add plants like chamomile to repel flying insects, chives to repel aphids, citronella to deter wild animals, and other such plants. Plan carefully if you want to use companion planting. Make sure that the plants you have chosen will grow well together and be beneficial to each other. Take a look at your list of plants you want to grow. Are there any that would benefit from companion planting?

Container Gardening

This is an excellent growing method to use if you have limited space, you want to have the freedom to move your plants around, or if you want to grow some of your plants indoors. The best thing about container gardening is that it increases your capacity to grow different kinds of plants.

For instance, if you discover that the soil on your land doesn't contain enough nutrients, you can still grow different kinds of plants in containers. Or if your land doesn't have any shade and the plants you want to grow require shade, you can always bring your plants (in their containers) indoors whenever the sun is high and it's too hot. The same thing goes for when you want to plant crops that won't thrive during the winter season. In such a case, you can simply move your plants inside your house or into a shed (if you have one) to protect them from the cold weather. If you choose container gardening, here are some considerations to keep in mind:

- You don't have to buy containers for your plants. Instead, you can 'upcycle,' which involves using other containers like cans or boxes to grow your plants. Just make sure to drill or punch holes at the bottoms of the containers to allow water to drain well.

- Even though you will grow plants in containers, still consider the placements and arrangements of the plants in your mini farm.

- Choose containers of the right size. Remember that the root systems of plants can grow big. If you want your plants to thrive, place them in appropriately sized containers.

- Don't forget to water your plants regularly as plants that grow in containers tend to dry out faster than plants that grow in the ground.

You can also grow ornamental plants in containers to beautify your mini farm or your home.

Hydroponics

This growing method doesn't involve the use of soil. Instead, you would grow your plants in containers filled with water. Then you would add nutrients to the water to keep your plants nourished. You can also place your plants in a growing medium like gravel, perlite, or coconut coir to support their growth. Hydroponics is quite complex as it involves a whole growing system that includes a water tank, containers for your plants, a water pump, tubes, and even a timer if you want the system to be automated. But the great thing about this growing method is that you can grow different kinds of plants—from herbs and microgreens to full-sized crops.

Intercropping

This growing method requires a lot of research and strategic planning. Here, you will grow fast-growing and slow-growing plants together on your farm. There are certain plants like potatoes and tomatoes that only need a lot of space when they have reached maturity. Until then, you can plant fast-growing plants such as salad leaves, beets, or radishes around or beside the slow-growing ones. Then you can harvest the fast-growing plants even before your slow-growing plants mature, which would also be the time when they would need more space.

Keyhole Gardening

This is another growing method that allows you to maximize the space in your garden. For this growing method, you need to arrange your plants in a circular shape with raised-style beds. Place this mini garden around a path shaped like a keyhole wherein the path will give you access to the whole garden. Right in the middle, you will place a vertical tunnel that contains several compost layers. Over time, the compost will break down, then provide moisture and nutrients to the plants on the raised beds.

You can construct this type of garden using various materials including bricks, corrugated sliding, landscaping rock, and more. If you have enough space on your land for a large circle plus a pathway around it, you may consider building a keyhole garden. If you are interested in this gardening method, a simple online search will give you more information about building the garden itself.

Lasagna Gardening

This is a unique growing method that doesn't require any digging. Also called "sheet composting," this method allows you to use all of your organic waste (food scraps, yard waste, and more) instead of throwing it away. It is also an eco-friendly way to grow organic crops for yourself, your family, and maybe even the people in your community. This gardening method involves planting in layers of root barriers, mulch, soil, and organic waste above the grass on your land. Therefore, you will be using the nutrients that are already present in the ground. But the most significant downside of this method is that the organic layers would also promote the growth of weeds. So you have to be very vigilant if you choose to use lasagna gardening.

Raised Bed Gardening

If you have a big piece of land and you want to plant a lot of crops, you may consider growing your plants on raised beds. This gardening method accommodates more plants and even reduces the occurrence of weeds. Even if weeds grow in your raised beds, it will be a lot easier for you to pull the weeds out compared to when they are growing in the ground. Growing your plants in raised beds offer many advantages including:

- You can grow your plants anywhere as long as the raised beds can fit in the space.
- Longer growing seasons.

- Maintaining and working the soil is much easier as you won't have to deal with soil compaction.
- Excellent drainage no matter what type of soil you use.

It will also be easier for you to tend to your plants as you won't have to bend over to reach your plants.

Succession Planting

This growing method allows you to harvest throughout the year. It's also ideal if you don't have a lot of space in your garden. For this method, you would be planting crops one after the other. Usually, you would plant quick-growing plants every 2 to 3 weeks throughout the growing season. Then the plants would mature at different times, which means that you will always have fresh produce to harvest.

Vertical Gardening

Another space-saving method, vertical gardening involves growing your plants in a vertical arrangement. You can do this by using pallet planters, trellises, and other supports for your plants to grow on. Planting crops on vertical trays beautifies your wall while giving you fresh produce to harvest. You can plant different types of crops in a vertical garden such as tomatoes, melons, winter squash, beans, peas, salad greens, strawberries, and even potatoes! The key here is to find the right containers and provide the right type of support to your growing plants. You can even plant in hanging containers and baskets where the plants will grow upside-down.

If you plan to use vertical farming, you would have to manage the humidity, temperature, and lighting. If needed, you may use artificial lighting for your plants to grow and thrive. You will also have to monitor and control the fertilizer and nutrients of your plants so that they will grow healthily. The viability of vertical gardening depends on the physical layout you have planned, the growing medium you use, and the sustainability features like wind turbines or rainwater tanks, for example.

As you can see, there are many growing methods you can use for your mini farm. To determine which method to use, you need to think about your needs and the plants you want to grow. Then you can choose the growing method that appeals to you the most so that you can start learning more about it.

Tips for Extending the Growing Seasons of Your Produce

Before you start growing your plants, you'll want to know how to make the most of each of the plants that you grow. This is especially important if you want to have a sustainable source of food for yourself and your family. To do this, you can try to extend the growing seasons of your crops. There are different ways to do this.

Water Your Plants Regularly

All plants need water to survive, including plants that produce fruits and vegetables. If your plants don't have enough water, their growth will slow down significantly. You might not even be able to harvest them when you expect to. If you want bountiful harvests and longer growing seasons, water your plants regularly. The soil should always be moist but not soaked so that your plants will produce high-quality crops.

Keep Nourishing Them Too

Apart from providing enough water to your plants, you should also nourish them with organic fertilizers as needed. You can either buy fertilizers for your plants or make your own compost. Keep checking your plants so that you can see if they are still healthy or if they need a nutrient boost to keep them going.

Pruning Is Essential

Pruning is an important part of caring for plants. But did you know that doing this can lengthen your plants' growing seasons too? When plants grow and thrive, they tend to cast shade over the garden. Unfortunately, when this happens, the crops that grow under these plants won't get enough sunshine and air. Pruning your plants regularly helps the sunlight pass through, which will ensure the health of all the plants on your farm.

Harvest Regularly

This is especially important for pod-producing vegetables and any type of fruit. If you keep harvesting, these plants will keep growing. The reason for this is that when pods and fruits ripen on the plants and form seeds, it signifies that the plants have completed their entire lifecycle. When this happens, your plants won't have any reason to continue bearing fruit. So if you have these kinds of plants on your farm, make sure to harvest regularly. The best part is, you will frequently have fresh harvests to enjoy!

Keep Your Plants Warm

Many plants cannot thrive when the weather gets too cold. If you want to extend the growing seasons of your plants even by just one to two weeks, consider adding floating row covers that will provide thermal comfort to your plants. A floating row cover is a woven or spun-bonded material that you would place over your plants. It's protective and it also retains heat without preventing air, water, and light from passing through. During the day, you can expose your plants to the air to allow for pollination. When the sun sets and it starts getting chilly, keep your plants covered.

You can also consider using cold frames, which are small greenhouses that are either stationary or mobile. These have bases made of wood that are low to the ground and transparent tops that you can open and close as needed. You can easily make your own cold frames using plastic or glass or buy them from gardening shops in your locale. You can use cold frames to protect your plants from the winter cold or during the spring season when there are occasional cold snaps.

Choose Your Plants Carefully

Another way to make sure that your growing season lasts longer is to choose the right plants and the right season to plant them. Often, it's much harder to grow plants during cold months, but there are certain species that can survive in cooler temperatures. Generally, crops that should be planted during the spring season can also be planted in the middle of summer. That way, you can still have produce to harvest even during the fall.

There are also late-season vegetables like carrots, spinach, salad greens, peas, beans, cabbage, and radishes that grow rapidly when planted during the later part of the summer. Since the temperatures will start to drop, this prevents the plants from going to seed. They can tolerate cold weather but it is still recommended to harvest before they succumb to frost. Of course, there are also cold-hardy plants that can survive during the winter. Plants such as kale, broccoli, turnips, beets, Brussels sprouts, and the like can be planted at the end of the growing seasons of your other plants so that you can still have produce to harvest during the winter season.

Crop Rotation

Rotating your crops will help extend your growing season while maintaining the health of your entire garden. This involves moving your crops from one location to another as the seasons change. Another benefit of crop rotation is that it reduces the risk of plant diseases and pests. Since you will be digging up your plants, the soil on your land will become more balanced too. By doing this, you will notice that your plants produce for longer time periods while growing more vigorously too.

Bring Your Plants Inside the House

If you have chosen to grow your plants in containers, another thing you can do is to grow your plants indoors when the weather is harsh outside. Just make sure that your plants get enough sunlight too. You can either bring your plants outside every morning, then bring them back in before the sun gets too hot or you can install artificial lighting around your plants. Many types of fruits and vegetables grow well indoors as long as you keep monitoring them and giving them what they need to thrive.

Keep Your Garden Clean

Finally, it's important to keep your garden clean all the time. To ensure a better and longer harvest, make sure that your plants are free of weeds and unnecessary material. You shouldn't leave any diseased plant materials, rotting leaves, or other debris on your fruit or vegetable beds.

This will promote pest infestation and block sunlight, which, in turn, slows down or stops the growth of your plants. Instead, add fallen leaves to the compost bin or pile so they can add carbon to the compost.

Maintenance Tips Throughout the Seasons

If you want to have bountiful harvests throughout the year, then you should learn how to care for your plants no matter what the season is. Different plants thrive in different seasons but you can also keep your plants healthy even if it's not their ideal season. With the right knowledge, you can become a successful farmer all year round.

Come Up With a Plan

First off, you need a plan for how you will care for your plants. You'll need to know which of your plants will grow and thrive during summer, spring, fall, and winter, and which of them will need extra care during certain seasons. Go through the list of plants you've made and write down the best time of year for planting each of them. (See chapters 5 and 6 for some planting times for specific plants and trees). Having a plan that contains all of these details will make it easier for you to keep your plants healthy all the time.

Make Sure Your Plants Get Enough Sunlight

All plants need sunlight to grow and stay healthy. But the sunlight that plants can get varies from one season to another. For instance, during the summer, the days can get very hot. So if you have plants that shouldn't be exposed to direct sunlight all the time, you should either provide shade for them or bring them inside your home. Or during the winter, when the weather gets too cold, you should find a way to warm up your plants so that they don't succumb to frost. If needed, you can use artificial light to keep your plants healthy even if the sun doesn't come out.

Fertilize as Needed

The nutrient needs of plants also vary throughout the seasons. When plants are still starting out or they are in the process of flowering, you can nourish them with fertilizer if you think that they aren't growing as well as they should. But if you see that your plants are thriving (especially if you regularly add mulch or compost), then you might not need to use fertilizer. The type of fertilizer—dry, organic, controlled-release, liquid, water-soluble, and more—will also depend on the plants you are growing. Generally, fertilizers come with their own plant recommendations. Of course, this only applies if you choose to buy fertilizers instead of making them yourself.

Weed Regularly

No matter what the season is, removing weeds is of the essence. Pull out or hoe any weeds as soon as you see them. It's much easier to pull out small weeds instead of fully-grown weeds that have already seeded. You can add mulch to your soil if you want to suppress the growth of seeds too. Weeds promote disease and pests, which is why keeping your garden free of them is important. While you're at it, if you see any crowded seedlings, dig them out and plant them somewhere else to give your plants space to grow.

Protecting Your Plants From Pests and Diseases

When it comes to growing plants, two of the biggest challenges you might have to deal with are pests and diseases. If you want to have a successful garden, you need to learn how to handle these issues.

Attract Pollinators and Other Beneficial Insects

One of the best ways to prevent or get rid of pests in your garden is by attracting beneficial insects to it. Such insects won't just eat the harmful pests but they will also act as pollinators for your plants. Some examples of beneficial insects are dragonflies, butterflies, ladybugs, hoverflies, praying mantises, and, of course, bees. If you can attract bats to your backyard garden, that would also be beneficial because they like to eat harmful insects. By using the tips mentioned above like keeping your garden clean, you can also prevent pest infestations. Here are other additional tips for keeping those pests away.

Find the Right Timing

If you're still in the planning stage, you can think about the best time to plant your crops. You should know that certain insects tend to appear in gardens at the same time each year. If you want to avoid infestations, you can set your planting schedule away from the heaviest feeding stages. These are the times when you will encounter very many pests that will cause harm to your plants. But you can only do this after observing your own garden for at least a year. Make note of the times when you see many pests on your plants and the times when you hardly see any creepy crawlies anywhere.

Put Plant Collars Around Your Plants

Plant collars are circular pieces of cardboard that you place on the base of your plants. This is an excellent option if you see that you have a cutworm infestation as the plant collars prevent these insects from reaching the bottoms of your plants where they feed.

Consider Using Organic Sprays

One important benefit of having your own mini garden is enjoying fresh produce grown without the use of pesticides and chemicals. If you feel like your pest infestation has gotten out of hand, you may opt for organic sprays. Instead of buying chemical-filled pesticides, you can make your own mineral oils, garlic sprays, salt sprays, and more. These will keep your plants protected without causing harm to you when you harvest and eat your crops.

Remove Bugs You Can See

While you are tending to your garden, you might notice some bugs munching on the leaves of your plants. Some bugs are easier to spot than others. If you see these insects, you should remove them right away. This will reduce the risk of pest infestations, specifically larger pests. Some examples of pests you can easily pick out from your garden are squash bugs, Japanese beetles, slugs, and cabbage worms. If you see any of these, remove them right away!

Spray Your Plants With Cold or Soapy Water

Spraying your plants with cold water can temporarily get rid of mites, aphids, and other pests. Cold water will make these bugs lose their grip on your plants and move away from your garden. Aside from cold water, you can also use soapy water either on its own or mixed with other ingredients such as:

- Baking soda and vinegar
- Pepper
- Milk

These simple, organic pesticides work wonders for pest control without compromising the quality of your crops.

Add Obstacles

You can also make it more challenging for pests to invade your garden by adding some obstacles to it. For instance, sprinkling crushed eggshells will make it challenging for pests like slugs to reach your plants as they travel on the soil. You can also plant herbs with strong aromas that deter pests such as basil, citronella, mint, fennel, and lemongrass.

Cover Your Plants With a Net

When you think of plant pests, you might immediately picture different types of insects. But these aren't the only type of organisms to look out for. Often, you might have to deal with bigger pests too, especially if you are growing fruits in your garden. Small animals like birds and squirrels can do a lot of harm to your plants, especially when harvest time approaches. To prevent these critters from reaching your plants, you can cover them with a net. This will keep small animals away while still allowing sunlight and air to reach your plants.

Build a Fence Around Your Garden

If you live in an area where there is much local wildlife, you might have to deal with bigger 'pests' like rabbits or deer. To prevent such animals from getting into your garden and eating your plants, you should build a fence around it. When these animals realize that they cannot access your plants, they will search for other food sources.

Never Crowd Your Plants

When it comes to preventing plant diseases, one of the best ways to do this is by having enough space between your plants. Air circulation is essential for the health of your plants. If there isn't enough airflow, this can result in various diseases.

Grow Resistant Plants

There are certain plants with pest- and disease-resistant characteristics. If you don't want to deal with pests or diseases, then you should choose these resistant plants for your garden. If you are starting from seeds you've bought, the labels of seed packets usually give an indication if the plants have these characteristics. You can also ask your local plant suppliers about the most resistant plant varieties.

Remove Any Diseased Plants

While you are gardening, if you see any plants or plant parts that are already diseased or have been consumed by pests, remove them. Plants like these are no longer healthy. If you keep them next to your healthy plants, they will end up destroying them. After removing the diseased plants or plant parts, throw them away. Don't add them to your compost pile as they will spread disease or pests into the rest of the organic materials. Then when you use the infected compost on your plants, they will all end up suffering.

Make Sure the Foliage Is Always Dry

Another common reason plants get infected with diseases is that their foliage is wet for too long. Therefore, it's best to water your plants in the morning so that the foliage will dry off thoroughly for the rest of the day.

Make Sure Your Plants Are Healthy

Of course, if you have healthy plants, they won't be susceptible to pests and diseases. As long as you are caring for your plants regularly and you maintain the cleanliness of your garden, you won't have to worry about dealing with these issues.

Chapter 5:

Growing Vegetables, Herbs, and Spices in Your Backyard Mini Farm

Now that you probably have a pretty good idea of which types of vegetables you'd like to grow, you're ready to get into the details. This chapter will give you some specific information for certain plants, like when it's best to grow them, and in what conditions they thrive best. This information can also help you choose which vegetables to grow if you're still unsure or are having trouble deciding. If you're a beginner, it's always best to start with crops that grow easily so that you will feel motivated to keep going.

What Vegetables Should You Grow in Your Garden?

When it comes to vegetables, there are tons of options for you to choose from. Even if you are a beginner, you can have a diverse veggie plantation even though it's small. Let's go through some tips for growing specific vegetables that will make it easier for you to start.

Beetroot

This is one of the easiest root vegetables to grow. You can boil beetroot and eat it as-is or add it to salads for a nutritional boost. You can sow beetroot seeds directly into moist soil, and the best months to plant this vegetable are between March and July. As the plants grow, thin the seedlings to avoid crowding. From the months of May to September (depending on when you planted your beetroots), you will already have colorful and succulent beetroots to harvest.

Bell Peppers

This is a versatile vegetable that adds color, texture, and nutrition to various dishes. It's very easy to grow bell peppers and it's recommended to start them indoors. Plant the seeds in a container, then keep them inside your home for about 4 to 6 weeks before transplanting them into your garden. Just remember that bell peppers thrive in the sun so it's best to plant them after the winter frost passes. You should also place your bell pepper plants in an area where they are exposed to direct sunlight all day. Plant the seeds in well-drained soil and fertilize them using compost. In a couple of months, you will already see lovely bell peppers growing on your plants.

Broad Beans

These beans are best planted during the spring season in small pots. Grow them from seeds in tiny containers and after a few weeks, you can plant them in your garden. Broad beans are sturdy plants that attract pollinators, especially when they start flowering. If you plant these beans in spring, you will already be able to harvest starting in June. And the flavor of broad beans grown in your garden is much more intense than the ones you will buy in any supermarket.

Carrots

This vegetable is very common and it is eaten by people from all over the world. Carrots are root vegetables that grow well in loose and sandy soil. The best time to plant carrots is during spring or fall. They are quite tolerant of cold and can even survive winter frost. Carrots are one type of vegetable that is relatively resistant to pests and diseases. If you harvest your carrots and you see that they are either deformed or short, it might be due to poor soil with rocks. Make sure the soil is loose and it drains well if you want to grow healthy and visually appealing carrot plants. You can also thin the seedlings when they start growing to avoid overcrowding your plants.

Cucumbers

While this veggie is easy to grow, you need to prepare your soil. Cucumbers need fertilizers that are high in potassium and nitrogen, especially if you want your plant to produce large yields. Cucumber plants are climbers so it's best to plant them near a fence. The fence will serve as the support for your cucumber plants while providing shelter too. It's also ideal to plant cucumbers next to corn (companion planting) so that the corn plants will trap heat, which will be beneficial for your cucumbers.

Green Beans

This is one veggie that will grow even if you plant it in poor soil. The reason for this is that green beans have the ability to fix nitrogen while growing. If you are planting the pole variety of green beans, make sure to plant them next to a trellis so that they can climb. If you plan to grow the bush variety, you don't need this support. If you live in a cool area, it's recommended to grow snap peas. But if you live in a warm area, it's recommended to grow southern peas or lima beans. No matter what you choose, green beans grow rapidly and thrive in moist, warm soil.

Microgreens

If you want to grow a veggie that you can harvest quickly, this is the best choice for you. Microgreens are simply young versions of certain plants—like mustard, basil, kale, broccoli, and more—before they grow into mature plants. Microgreens are rich in nutrition, they are very flavorful, and they only take a couple of weeks to grow. As the name implies, microgreens are small plants, which means that they don't need a lot of space. You can start growing your microgreens indoors in trays or other containers or you can grow them in your garden. If you plan to expand your farm and start earning, microgreens can be one of the many fresh vegetables you offer to your potential customers.

Mushrooms

While a lot of people don't include mushrooms in their mini farm plans, you should consider growing these fungi. You can grow mushrooms in vertical spaces and they will produce high yields for you. Mushrooms have quick growing cycles, which means that you can harvest them often. You can buy mushroom kits that already contain everything you need to grow them. However, these take a bit more time and effort to maintain compared to the other veggies listed here.

Onions and Garlic

The great thing about these crops is that they are virtually maintenance-free. They are so easy to grow that you can even include them in your list of veggies as an afterthought! Since onions and garlic are very versatile, having a constant supply would be very beneficial for you. Just plant garlic cloves or onion bulbs into the soil during spring or fall, then wait for them to grow. When summertime comes and the foliage of these plants turns yellow, you can harvest them. Then store them in your kitchen for when you need to add them to your dishes.

Peas

This is another easy crop to grow and it thrives in cool weather. Sow the peas right into the ground between the months of March and June so that you can enjoy sweet and fresh peas between June to August. Just make sure to add some netting or chicken wire to support the stems of the plants as they grow bigger.

Potatoes

The best time to grow potatoes is between the months of February and March. Partially fill a potato bag with soil and compost, then leave the potatoes to grow. When you see the green shoots coming out of the soil, use more compost to cover them. Don't forget to water the potato plants too. Continue doing this until you have filled the bag. About 10 to 20 weeks after planting, you will notice that the foliage will start turning yellow. This is when you know that the potatoes are ready to harvest.

Radishes

This crunchy vegetable with a peppery taste is easy to grow in the ground or in containers. You can plant radishes throughout the summer season to have a continuous harvest to enjoy. Sow the seeds of radishes spaced about one inch apart in loose soil. Cover them completely, then water regularly. You can keep planting radish seeds every ten days or so, then thin the seedlings as soon as they start sprouting.

Runner Beans

Just like broad beans, you can sow runner bean seeds during the summer. Just remember that these plants are climbers. You need to provide them with a lot of support and space as they are growing. Water your runner beans well to enjoy a constant harvest. It's important to harvest regularly to ensure that your runner beans stay healthy.

Salad Leaves

Different kinds of salad leaves like lettuce, kale, cabbage, spinach, and more are easy to grow too. It's best to sow the seeds of these greens during the summer so that you can enjoy your harvests about 3 weeks later. And the best part is, these plants will keep on growing as long as you keep harvesting.

Summer Squash and Zucchini

These plants are quite easy to grow in well-composted soil. You should also give them a lot of sun and a lot of space to grow. Water the soil regularly making sure to keep the foliage dry. When the vegetables are ripe, you can harvest and enjoy them!

Tomatoes

Tomatoes are so easy to grow that you can even invite children to grow them with you. Plant tomatoes in the ground, in small containers placed on the windowsill, or even in hanging baskets. Just keep watering your tomato plants and watch them grow! If needed, add some support while the plants are growing to keep the stems from breaking.

As you can see, there are many veggies you can grow on your farm even if this is your first time. Practice your gardening skills with these plants, then you can opt for more challenging plants once you have mastered the basics.

What Herbs and Spices Should You Grow in Your Garden?

Apart from vegetables, you can also start growing herbs and spices in your garden. These will be wonderful additions to your mini farm as they can be added to various dishes. Herbs and spices make food more flavorful and they also add a boost of nutrition to all of your meals. You can grow herbs in your garden or have a small indoor herb garden in your kitchen. Either way, if you want to grow these nutrient-dense plants, you can start with these.

Basil

This is a very popular herb that you can grow from seeds. If you want to have a constant supply of basil, you can plant the seeds every 3 to 4 weeks until the frost of winter comes. The great thing about basil is that basil flowers bloom from mature plants and these flowers will attract pollinators like bees to your garden.

Bay Laurel

This plant has thick leaves that add a delicious flavor to dishes. Plant this in soil that drains rapidly and place the plant in direct sunlight for it to thrive. You should also make sure that there is enough circulation of air so that your bay laurel plants won't succumb to disease. When harvesting, remember that bigger, more mature leaves have a stronger flavor.

Cilantro, Parsley, and Dill

These herbs prefer cool weather and they might not survive during the hot days of the summer. It's best to plant them during the fall so that you can harvest when spring comes. They are quite tolerant to cold, which means that they can survive the winter season even if you grow them outside.

Chervil

This is a common herb in France and it has a parsley-anise-like flavor. Plant the seeds in a deep pot filled with moist potting soil. Once the plants have sprouted, provide them with moderate sand. If you want to have a steady supply of chervil leaves, keep replanting every couple of weeks.

Chives and Garlic Chives

These herbs grow from tiny bulbs and you can eat their flowers and leaves. If you want these plants to continue growing, don't harvest the flowers. That way, they will seed and self-sow in your garden.

Cumin

This plant loves heat and it's growing season lasts between 3 to 4 months. If you want the plant to seed, make sure to water it regularly. The plant will produce white-pink flowers. When these flowers are done blooming, you will already be able to harvest the brown seeds, which you can use in your cooking.

Fennel

This plant belongs to the same family as cumin and it tastes like licorice or anise. Sow the seeds in your garden directly since fennel doesn't thrive when transplanted. It's best to grow this plant in a sunny place with moderately fertile, well-draining soil. If you want to make the most of this spice, allow the plant to flower and go to seed. You can even munch on the fennel seeds to improve your digestion.

Fenugreek

This aromatic spice can easily be grown in the ground or in containers. Plant it in well-draining soil that's amended with compost. Plant the seeds directly in your garden after the winter frost. The seeds are usually ready to harvest during the fall.

Mint

There are so many types of mint varieties to choose from that you can fill an entire section of your garden with different mint plants. This herb will thrive in moist soil with moderate to strong sunlight. They are hardy plants that produce fragrant stems. They are visually appealing too.

Mustard

This herb is best planted in the early part of spring. In hot conditions, it doesn't do well, and it will seed right away, which means it won't produce a quality harvest. Grow mustard plants in compost-amended soil and water them regularly. When you see small white or yellow flowers, leave them alone. You can pick the pods once they have turned brown.

Oregano, Thyme, Sweet Marjoram, and Sage

These are very common herbs that can be used in different dishes, so planting them in your garden will be highly beneficial to you. These plants need a lot of sun and well-draining soil to thrive. When the plants are mature, you can start harvesting the leaves.

Rosemary

This is a drought-tolerant herb that's quite easy to grow. It can also tolerate the hot and sunny days of summer, as well as the cool temperatures of winter. Just make sure that your rosemary plants get enough sun for them to grow well.

Turmeric and Ginger

These are two of the healthiest spices in the world so you should include them in your garden too. Plant turmeric or ginger directly in the ground or in containers. These are both root crops that need consistent moisture and partial shade to thrive. However, they take between 8 to 10 months to mature before you can start harvesting them.

Now that you've learned some details on planting specific vegetables, herbs, and spices, it's time to move on to growing fruits.

Chapter 6:

Growing Fruits in Your Backyard

Mini Farm

Have you ever tried picking a piece of fruit from a tree?

There is something so satisfying about growing your own fruit trees and being able to pick the fruits when they are ripe. You can even make a profit if you can choose the right fruits that the people in your community (or your potential customers) are looking for.

Growing Fruit Trees

It might seem quite overwhelming to grow a tree on your farm, especially when you think about how much space they need. However, these days, you can grow smaller versions of the most common fruit trees so that they will fit onto your mini farm.

When choosing the type of tree to grow in your garden, it's best to go to a local garden shop. That way, you can ask for advice from the supplier on what would be the best choice for you. Or if you already have a specific tree in mind, you can ask your local supplier if it's possible to grow that tree on your farm and some tips for how you can do this. It's also a good idea to ask if you need to buy more than just a single tree for your farm. For instance, fruit trees like peaches or cherries are self-fertile, which means that they will bear fruit even if you only have a single tree. But fruit trees like pears and apples require a 'partner' growing next to them so that they can pollinate and bear fruits. This is something you should ask your supplier before buying.

You can grow trees whether in pots or in the ground. If you choose the former, make sure that the container you will grow your trees in is deep enough and has drainage holes at the bottom. Use a soil-based potting mix that will release nutrients gradually since it takes time for trees to grow. It's also recommended to place your trees in locations where they will get a lot of sunlight so that they will grow well. Of course, you should also water your trees regularly to keep them healthy. While all trees require pruning, the amount and method of pruning vary from one tree to another. This is another thing you should ask your local supplier about when you are buying trees for your mini farm. If you would like to include some fruit trees in your mini farm, you have a lot of options to choose from.

Apple Trees

When you think of fruit trees, one of the first ones that will come to your mind is apple trees. If you would like to challenge yourself and improve your gardening skills, this is a great option. Apple trees are susceptible to several diseases and pest infestations. Although this tree is quite hardy, you would still have to apply various protection methods to keep them healthy. It's also essential to prune apple trees regularly, focusing on thinning branches so that air and sunlight can reach all the parts of the tree. You can grow apple trees either in containers or in the ground. If you don't have a lot of space, opt for one of the dwarf varieties.

Apricot Trees

It's easy to grow apricot trees in a garden since this is a self-fertilizing tree. You only need to plant one apricot tree and get the assurance that it will bear fresh fruits. These trees will grow well in direct sunlight, but they will also survive in cool temperatures. You can opt for dwarf varieties if you don't have a lot of space in your garden or you can also opt for a full-sized tree. Either way, it's recommended to purchase a tree that's already a year old so that its root system is already developed.

Cherry Trees

This is another type of tree that's easy to grow and maintain. Cherry trees don't require a lot of pruning. But if you will prune your tree, do it during the winter as this is the season when the tree is dormant. Cherry trees are relatively resistant to diseases and pests and they're tolerant to drought too. If you want to harvest sweet cherries from your tree, make sure to get a pair of trees. If you don't mind sour cherries, which can be used for baking, one tree would be enough.

Fig Trees

You can grow a fig tree directly in your garden or in a container. Fig trees are relatively pest-resistant and they don't need to be pruned often. There are several varieties of fig trees, most of which are very hardy. If you want to grow a small tree, plant it in a small container, and make sure to bring the tree indoors when the winter starts so that the tree will remain healthy.

Kaffir Lime Trees

The fruits, flowers, and even the leaves of this tree are very fragrant, making them a wonderful addition to your mini farm. It's easy to grow Kaffir lime trees, especially the dwarf varieties. These trees are self-pollinating too, which means that you can expect to harvest even with a single tree. They also attract pollinators thanks to their sweet scent. Just make sure to protect your Kaffir lime trees from frost as they are very sensitive to the cold.

Kumquat Trees

If you live in an area with a warm climate, consider adding kumquat trees to your mini farm. These trees are naturally compact and they bear fruit during the fall and spring seasons. You can easily grow kumquat trees in containers and it's recommended to bring them indoors during the winter season.

Lemon Trees

Lemon trees grow tall, which makes them a great addition to your backyard farm if you want something that will provide shade. If you grow a lemon tree, you will have to prune it regularly so that you can find and pick the fruits easily. This is also recommended if you don't want your lemon tree to grow too big. Lemon trees grow best in areas with low humidity and they have long growing seasons.

Peach Trees

Peach trees are relatively small, making them perfect for a mini farm, and they are easy to grow. You only have to prune occasionally to promote fruiting and prevent the tree from growing too big. When you thin the tree while it's still young, it will produce few but large crops. Otherwise, the tree will produce a lot of tiny peaches. Pruning is also essential to allow good airflow and adequate sunlight to reach all the parts of the tree.

Pear Trees

The great thing about pear trees is that they are fairly resistant to pests and diseases. But they aren't self-pollinating, which means that you need to grow at least two pear trees if you want to enjoy fresh fruits. Grow pear trees in well-draining soil, direct sunlight, and good air circulation. You should also prune them at least once every year. These trees are slow starters and you would have to wait for about three years or so before you will see them bear fruit. But once they do, pear trees will bear fruits for several years.

These are just some examples that show how you can plant different kinds of fruit trees on your mini farm. If you want to plant more than one variety of tree, make sure to plan the placement well.

Growing Other Kinds of Fruits

If you don't think that fruit trees will fit in your mini farm but still want to have a constant supply of fresh fruits, consider growing other types of fruit-bearing plants. These plants won't just give you something sweet to enjoy, they will also be beautiful additions to your backyard farm.

Blueberries

Blueberries grow on shrubs. They change each season and each stage is wonderful. During the spring, blueberry shrubs grow white flowers. When summer comes, you can harvest fresh blueberries. And during the fall, the foliage turns a gorgeous red color. Before you grow blueberry plants, you need to make the soil acidic first by adding compost, leaf mold, sulfur, pine needle mulch, and other materials that promote acidity. If you can establish a healthy blueberry shrub (or a few of them), they will produce fresh fruits for several years.

Caneberries

Raspberries and blackberries are types of caneberries that also grow on shrubs. Pruning is essential for these plants. The pruning method you would use depends on the variety of caneberries you will grow. For instance, if you will grow primocane fruiting raspberries, you can prune them completely after fruiting. But if you will grow a variety of trailing blackberries, you need to remove the fruited and dead canes while pruning. Once you decide the variety to grow, learn more about how to prune it properly.

Currants

You can grow currant plants in small containers, tight spaces, and even in your garden. There are different colors of currants and you have the freedom to choose which variety to grow. Plant your currant plants in direct sunlight to enjoy large yields. However, you will have to wait a few years before your currant plant will start bearing fruits.

Dragon Fruits

Dragon fruits grow on vines and have aerial roots. This plant bears white-colored flowers during spring or summer, then bears the unique-looking fruit afterward. Dragon fruit vines are quite hardy, but you should know that they spread rapidly. If you would like to have plenty of vines, make sure you have a strong trellis for the plant to climb on.

Goji Berries

This is another fruit that's easy to grow. It's quite hardy as it can handle fast-draining soil and windy conditions without getting compromised. Just place your goji berry plant in a location that gets a lot of sun and watch it grow.

Gooseberries

This fruit grows in a deciduous plant and it bears high yields of different-colored fruits by the middle of the summer season. Gooseberry vines are tolerant of morning sunlight but prefer afternoon shade. Keep this in mind when thinking of the location where you will place this plant. Gooseberries are great for attracting butterflies, but they can also attract birds, so you may need to add protection, like draping netting over your plant so that birds cannot get to the fruits.

Grapes

This delicious fruit grows on vines that are easy to maintain. The only big issue is that when harvest time comes, the grapes will attract different types of animals. Since grapes grow on vines, you also need to place a trellis or another type of support for the plant to grow on. Pruning isn't done often with this plant. Just make sure that you plant it in well-draining, rich soil and in a sunny location that gets enough air.

Kiwis

This is another fruit that grows on deciduous vines. You will see clusters of white flowers with a subtle fragrance as the end of spring approaches, then the fruits will come during the early part of fall. Kiwi plants are quite hardy and are mostly resistant to diseases and pests.

Melons

Growing melons on your mini farm is easy, whether you plant them in the ground or in containers. Make sure to place your melon plants in a location with a lot of heat and sunlight. You also need to give them plenty of space and support for the vines to grow. If you want to grow melons vertically, choose a variety that produces small-sized fruits.

Passion Fruits

This fruit grows in a vine that produces colorful flowers. Passion fruit plants grow rapidly, especially in tropical countries. If you grow this plant in a container, bring it inside during the winter. Passion fruit vines will flourish when planted in well-draining soil and in a sunny location. You just have to wait for more than a year before you can harvest fresh fruits from this plant.

Pineapples

Surprising as this may seem, you can grow pineapples on your mini farm. Cut off the crown of a pineapple, then soak it in a shallow container for 24 hours. Then you can transfer the crown to a bigger container or outside to your garden. If you choose the former, you should place the container under direct sunlight. After some time, you will already have a full-grown fruit to enjoy. It's that simple!

Strawberries

The great thing about strawberry plants is that they keep bearing fruit every year. There are many varieties of strawberries to choose from and they are very easy to grow. Simply plant some 'runners' to root and start growing. Then water them regularly and keep monitoring their growth over time.

After you establish the garden on your farm and are already enjoying the fruits of your labor, it's time to make things more interesting.

Chapter 7:

Raising Animals on Your Mini

Farm

You've learned all about raising plants, but raising animals is a whole new ball game, and it comes with its own set of lessons for you to learn. Whether you want to make a profit from your farm or you just want to have a sustainable source of animal products in your backyard, making the choice to raise animals is a big one and means spending more time and effort on your mini farm. Just like plants, animals are living things too. And they often need much more attention.

That being said, raising animals on your mini farm can be extremely fulfilling. Each type of animal comes with its own unique challenges and successes. As you try your hand at raising animals on your mini farm, you will discover that this is a lifelong learning process that will make you a better backyard farmer.

Beginner Tips to Start With

Raising animals is a huge commitment, and there are several things you should think about and consider before you bring any animals onto your farm.

Determine if You Are Ready to Raise Animals

First and foremost, you need to determine if you are ready for such an endeavor. While you might have breezed through gardening, raising animals might be more of a challenge for you. The fact is, not everyone is cut out to raise animals. Even if you have enough space and a lot of enthusiasm, you should first consider your decision carefully. Before you make a decision, ask yourself the following questions:

- Why do you want to raise animals?
- Is there a reliable supplier in your locale (for equipment, food, and the animals themselves)?
- Do you have enough resources to support your animals even when they get sick?
- Are you ready to be on-call for your animals all day, every day?
- Do you know anyone who will be willing to care for your animals when you have to go away from your mini farm?

- If you plan to make a profit from raising animals, do you have a business plan?
- How comfortable are you (and the rest of your family members) with different kinds of animals?
- Do you have time to care for the animals while also tending to your plants and doing other chores around the house?
- Does your area have the right climate for the animals you have chosen? This is something you can't change so you need to consider this first.
- Do you have enough space for each of the animals you plan to raise?
- Is there a possible support system in your community (veterinarians, people who are currently raising different types of animals, and the like) that can help you deal with any issues if they arise?

Make Sure You Have All of the Requirements

If you've answered the above questions and still feel confident that you will be able to raise animals, you're ready to move on to the next step in the planning phase—making sure you have everything the animals will require. These include:

- The right facilities to raise your animals.
- A habitat for the animals.
- A veterinarian who you can consult with if your animals get sick.
- Permits and other legal issues such as breeder permits or licenses.

It's also a good idea to do a lot of research before buying your first farm animal. You will learn more in the next chapter about raising specific farm animals, but you are also going to want to do your own research on animals you are considering raising, like looking for reputable producers and breeders in your area and talking to them about your plans. A great way to learn is always to talk to people who have already done it, so see if you can also find someone to talk to who is raising the particular animals you are interested in. You can even join forums where you can ask questions to learn more. Educating yourself is essential, especially if you want this addition to your farm to be a success.

Set a Budget

It's also important for you to consider the cost of raising animals. You need to spend for the habitat, facilities, the transport needed to bring the animals to your home, feed, vaccinations (for some types of animals) and other vet expenses, and the animals themselves. Ask around your locale to find out if it's possible for you to add animals to your farm. Then you can come up with a realistic budget, which you should then stick to as much as possible.

Decide the Type of Animals to Raise

Now comes the fun part...choosing which animals to raise, which we will explore in detail in the next chapter. There are many animals to choose from and your decision should also depend on your goal for raising animals in the first place. For instance, if you and your family love to eat chicken and eggs, consider raising poultry. If you want to have a steady supply of meat, you may choose cows, goats (both of which also give milk), or even pigs. You can even ask the rest of your family to help you decide. This decision is especially important if you plan to turn your mini farm into a business.

Raising animals on your mini farm is a commitment. Animals aren't something that you buy, place on your farm, and forget. They will need a lot of care and attention. Think of it as an investment, whether you plan to make money from your farm or not.

Chapter 8:

What Animals Can You Raise on

Your Backyard Mini Farm?

After making the choice to raise animals on your mini farm, it's time to start thinking about the types of animals to care for. You have many options to choose from, which is why it's important to reflect and research first before you make a final decision. If you've weighed the pros and cons and still feel ready to take on such a commitment, good for you! In this chapter, you will learn all about the different kinds of animals that could grow well on mini farms such as the one you are planning to have in your backyard.

Raising Livestock

When you think of farm animals, you probably picture goats, cows, horses, and chickens. Of course, you can opt for these animals, but there are others you can add to your mini farm too. The following is a list of common and not so common farm animals and some basic considerations on how to care for them.

Chickens

If you love eating eggs and chicken dishes, then raising chickens on your mini farm is an excellent option. Before buying chickens from a reputable supplier, you need to have an enclosure—like a coop—to shelter your chickens. Make sure that the enclosure is big enough for the number of chickens you plan to place in it. Having this is also important to prevent predators from devouring your chickens.

Simple as chickens might seem, they do need a lot of affection and mental stimulation. Keep this in mind if you plan to raise this animal. You can start your flock of chickens by purchasing day-old chicks. Or if you only want to raise chickens for the purpose of having eggs, you should purchase young hens (point-of-lay pullets) that are already old enough to lay eggs. The latter is also an easier option if you have no experience raising farm animals. Either way, having an enclosure should be your first priority.

When it comes to feeding your chickens, you should know that grass-fed chickens lay tastier eggs and have tastier meat too. It's also important to have your chickens vaccinated to reduce their risk of getting poultry diseases.

Cows

If you have a lot of space on your farm, then you may consider raising cows. Cows can give you milk and later on, they can be slaughtered for their meat. But you will probably need to get a special permit first before you can buy a cow and raise it on your farm. You may get away with having one or two cows in your backyard, but if you want to have an entire herd—like if you have a lot of space—check if you're allowed to do this first. Laws vary, so make sure you research the laws in your specific locale, whether you plan to raise one or several cows.

Dogs

If you plan to raise several types of livestock, then you might also want to consider raising livestock guardian dogs such as Maremmas, Anatolian Shepherds, or Great Pyrenees. Herding dogs could also be beneficial on your farm to keep the other animals in line. Some examples of herding dogs are Border Collies, Australian Shepherds, and Australian Cattle Dogs.

Ducks

If you have a pond or some other body of water on your farm, why don't you raise some ducks? Even a small inflatable pool would be okay too. Apart from the body of water, you should also provide a safe and adequately sized enclosure for your ducks to protect them from predators and harsh weather. When it comes to ducks, you shouldn't overfeed them as this isn't healthy.

Geese

This farm animal is low-maintenance once it reaches maturity. When purchasing geese, you have two options. First, you can purchase goslings from a reputable hatchery. Just make sure that you know how to care for goslings and nurture them until they are fully grown (which is when they will be low-maintenance). Second, you can purchase adult geese, which are more expensive. If you're a beginner, this might be the easier choice.

Adult geese graze on their own and you only need to scatter some grains to increase the amount of food they have access to. Also, provide a water source for them to drink out of. Geese are tolerant to most types of weather but you still need to provide them with some kind of shelter with bedding, which is especially important during the winter season.

Goats

Before purchasing a goat from a breeder, make sure that you're allowed to have one on your farm first. As with any other farm animal, prepare an enclosure first. This will shelter your goat from the elements. It would be nice if the enclosure had several levels because goats love to climb and jump. Also, having fencing around your farm or the area where your goats will roam should be made of chain link or some other 'goat-proof' material so that they won't escape. In terms of food, you can allow your goats to graze on your farm (away from your fruits and vegetables, of course). Otherwise, you can provide bales of hay for your goats to munch on.

Horses

If you only have a mini farm in your backyard, you probably won't have enough space to house a whole herd of horses in a stable. But if you have a structure where you can keep horses, you might be able to add one or two to your mini farm. Just make sure that you're allowed to have these farm animals on your farm first. Horses need a lot of space to graze so you should consider this too. They also need a lot of space to run around to keep them healthy. You should also have a local veterinarian on call in case anything happens to your horses.

Llamas and Alpacas

While quite uncommon, you might want to raise llamas and alpacas on your farm too. These farm animals are considered investments since they can be sold for a good price. Apart from breeding and selling these animals, you can get high-quality fleece from them.

Pigs

If you want to raise companion animals on your farm, pigs are an excellent choice. Of course, you can enjoy pork if you choose to slaughter the pigs but you can also consider breeding and selling them. Just remember that pigs are quite messy and they will eat anything. If they get into your vegetable or fruit garden, they will eat your crops, so you need to have a housing enclosure and adequate fencing to prevent your pigs from wandering around. Confining pigs in one area also makes it easier to clean up their manure. You can add the manure you collect to your compost bin or even sell it as fertilizer to other farmers in your community.

Quail

If you don't have enough space to raise large farm animals, you may opt for quails. These birds are much quieter compared to chickens and they don't require a lot of space. Just make sure that you have prepared an adequate enclosure to keep them safe and confined in a single area.

Rabbits

Rabbits are also an excellent choice for mini farms. You can raise them outdoors or indoors. If you are growing vegetables in your garden, having a rabbit is especially beneficial because you can use their manure as fertilizer without having to compost it first. Rabbits are excellent companion animals too. You can keep them in a fenced enclosure or in a cage that's big enough for them to hop around in.

Sheep

These days, hair sheep are becoming very popular. This type of sheep sheds its fleece, which means that you don't have to go through the trouble of shearing. They also breed out of season, which means that you will have healthy lambs to sell when the demand rises. Even the industry of dairy sheep is on the rise as milk cheese from sheep is also growing in popularity. If hair sheep aren't your cup of tea, you have other options too including miniature sheep, heritage sheep, or even rarer breeds.

Turkeys

Farmers often raise turkeys for their meat and their eggs. If you plan to raise turkeys for their meat, heritage turkeys are the best choice. They have a wonderful flavor and lovely plumage too. But if you just want to raise turkeys for their eggs, opt for Beltsville Whites. Whichever type of turkey you decide to raise, keep in mind that these birds are much larger than chickens so the enclosure you make should be big enough to house them.

Remember to thoroughly prepare your mini farm first before adding any type of livestock to it. Also, research how to raise the animal you have chosen to ensure that you can grow them successfully, achieve your purpose, and gain the benefits too.

Beekeeping

If you love honey and you're interested in beekeeping, this could be another amazing addition to your mini farm. Beehives don't require a lot of space and setting up beehives isn't costly either. Spending around $500 should be enough for everything you will need, including the bees. You can build your own bee farm in your backyard, then cultivate your own honey supply. The great thing about beekeeping is that it offers many benefits apart from providing you with fresh honey. These include:

- You can harvest beeswax from the honeycombs of your bees, then use it for cosmetics or candle-making.
- You can also get royal jelly, propolis, and bee honey, which can be sold for high prices.
- Bees are pollinators so having them on your mini farm will be beneficial for your plants.

Of course, adding bees to your mini farm means that you will have to spend more time on your farm chores too. But this endeavor is very fulfilling and it can also be a lot of fun. As with raising livestock, there are some things you can do to make your efforts successful.

Learn About the Beekeeping Regulations in Your Locale

Before you start creating a plan or preparing for your beehive, you should first find out if beekeeping is allowed in your locale. When you have verified that you can raise bees on your mini farm, you can start with your preparations. First, you should buy safety gear. You will need this to protect yourself while you work with bees, especially if this is your first time doing so. Next, you should talk to your neighbors about your plans. Before you do this, you should do a lot of research about beekeeping. That way, you can give your neighbors the assurance that you know what you are doing and your hobby won't put them at risk of getting stung.

Find the Perfect Location and Prepare it

After your initial preparations, the next thing to do is to find the best location for your beehives. When choosing a location, remember that bees need:

- Sunlight.
- Afternoon shade, especially if you live in a hot area.
- A source of fresh and clean water near the beehive.
- Privacy, which means that you shouldn't place your beehive in an area where people, pets, or animals frequent.
- Some kind of protection above or around the beehive to protect the bees from wind or other extreme weather conditions.

It's best to position your beehive near a tall hedge or fence to limit contact with animals and people. You should also place your beehives in an elevated location to protect them from animals and dampness. Before buying your beehive, it's also recommended to build a tall fence around the area where you plan to place it.

Purchase or Build a Hive

After you have prepared the location, it's time to look for a hive. If you have good woodworking skills, you may opt to build the beehive. Otherwise, you can purchase one from your local supplier. Usually, beehives or their components are made of unfinished wood. Before adding your bees to them, you should paint or stain the wood to make them sturdier. This will also protect your bees from the cold winter weather. Either way, there are different types of hives you can choose from:

- A Langstroth is very common and is made up of supers (wooden boxes) that are stacked on top of one another.

- A top bar beehive looks like a trough.
- A warre is a bit smaller and looks like a combination of a top bar beehive and a hollowed-out tree.

If you want to save some money, you can try to look for used beehives too. Of course, these might not last as long as new ones but they can still be a viable option for you.

Purchase or Catch Your Bees

You read that right. You can catch the bees to keep in your beehive. But you should only do this if you discover that an entire swarm of bees has made its home somewhere on your property. The more common (and safer) option is to purchase bees from a reliable apiary. You can purchase a nuclear colony (a small colony taken from a bigger one) or a package of bees (with the queen bought separately). If you are a beginner, you may want to purchase 'gentle' types of bees such as Buckfast bees. These are easier to care for and they're great pollinators too.

Add the Bees

When your bees arrive at your home, you should first put on your safety gear. Then you can transfer the bees from the container they came in (which is usually a screened box) into your beehive. The best time to do this is during the spring season when there will be a lot of flowers that will serve as the food supply of your bees. If you bought your bees from an apiary, you should ask for tips on how to transfer them into your beehive.

Feed Your Bees

Young bee colonies need to care for their queen, their growing brood, and build their home. Even if you have a garden filled with flowers, you can provide more food for your bees by making homemade 'nectar.' Simply combine equal parts of water and granulated sugar, then place the mixture into small jars with feeder lids. Place the jars (inverted) into the holes of the beehive for the bees to feed on. Once you see that the colony is already established, you can stop providing this additional sustenance.

Check Your Bees and Hives Regularly

Once your bees have established their colonies, you don't have to do much anymore. However, it's important to check your bees and beehives regularly to make sure that everything is okay. Once a week, open the hives up, check the queen, and observe the other bees. It's also important to clean the surrounding areas of the beehive regularly. Remove any bee poop, litter, ants, and other pests. You should also check for varroa mite infestations in the hive. These are tiny insects that you can spot if you are observant enough. They are reddish or copperish brown and look like ticks. You can see them on the abdomens of the worker bees if you look closely. If you discover any issues during your inspection, seek help from your local apiologist right away.

When the weather is warm, you have to put in more time to care for your bees and harvest honey. But when the cold months start, the bees in your beehive will go dormant, which means that inspecting the hives will be your main concern. If you discover that beekeeping is something you're passionate about, you can start planning how to expand your beehive and maybe even include this in your business plan for the future.

Fish Farming

While caring for animals on land is fun and fulfilling, you can also choose to raise fish in an underwater environment. If you have a mini farm, you can either grow fish in a natural pond (if you have one on your land) or in a container. Just like with raising livestock and keeping bees, there are steps you need to take to start raising fish.

Determine the Type of Fish You Will Raise

The first thing you'll want to do is determine which type of fish you will raise. As a beginner, there are certain fish you can start with that are relatively easy to raise and are suitable to grow on a mini farm.

- **Catfish**

    This fish is a bottom feeder, it's very resilient, and it can survive in various water conditions. Catfish eat flake foods, pellets, frozen or live bloodworms, Mysis shrimp, and brine shrimp. But the preferences of this fish vary according to species. If you enjoy the unique flavor of catfish, you can raise this on your farm for food.

- **Koi or Carp**

  If you have a pond on your land, you may choose to raise koi, which are very resilient. They can survive even in hot summers and cold winters and they tend to grow big. Koi eats different types of insects, fruits, vegetables, fish food, and even cereal. Carp are similar to koi and they would be a better choice if you want to raise fish for food. Just make sure to check the regulations in your area as some carp varieties are considered invasive. In such a case, you might have to get a special permit to raise this fast-growing and tough fish. You can also raise these fish in containers.

- **Perch**

  There are different perch species that you can raise on your farm but the most common is the yellow perch. This variety grows rapidly and it thrives in cold water. So if you live in a cold area where the water is always cold, raising perch could be a good option for you.

- **Salmon**

  Salmon is one of the healthiest fish to eat. This fish survives in cold weather as long as the water is clean. Usually, salmon are raised from eggs instead of fingerlings or fry. So you might want to raise other types of fish first before attempting to raise salmon on your farm.

- **Striped Bass**

  This is the most common variety of bass that backyard farmers raise because it is fast-growing and quite hardy. Striped bass has a mild flavor and makes an excellent addition to your farm if you want to raise fish for food.

- **Tilapia**

  This is one of the more common types of fish that backyard farmers choose to raise as they can survive no matter what the weather is, but you do need to regulate the water temperature.

Make sure the temperature of the water is above 77°F. When the weather is cold, you may have to turn on the water heater in your pond or container to maintain the ideal temperature. Tilapia eat insects and plant-based foods. They also grow quickly, which is why farmers love them so much.

- **Trout**

  This is one type of fish that survives in cold weather. However, they are a bit picky when it comes to food so it's best to give them store-bought fish food meant for trout. This type of fish also needs clean water since they use their eyes instead of their sense of smell to find their food. If the water isn't clear, your fish might have a hard time finding their food.

No matter which fish you choose to raise, make sure to do your research first. Also, find a reputable fish supplier to get your fish from. That way, you can also ask them questions about raising the fish you have chosen.

Prepare the Habitat for Your Fish

After you've decided which type of fish you're going to raise, you will need to prepare their habitat, which can be relatively easy if you already have a small pond on your property. All you have to do here is take a quick inspection of your pond to make sure that it's suitable for growing fish. Then you can purchase fish and place them in the pond. Just make sure that the depth of your pond is at least 1.64 feet (half a meter) to avoid the growth of weeds and the risk of predators. When choosing fish for your pond, consider the size of your pond and the place you live in. Even if a pond is a natural habitat, you shouldn't add too many fish as they won't thrive when they are overcrowded. Another important thing to do is to install a water heater in your pond, especially if you know that the pond freezes over during the winter.

If you don't have a pond, you can raise your fish in containers. You can place them in aquariums, plastic tanks, and other similar containers. Once you have a container, fill it with water. Don't add any chemicals to the water as these might compromise the health of your fish. Also, make sure that the container is big enough for the number of fish that you plan to place in it.

Optimize the Ecosystem

If you want your fish to thrive, whether in a pond or a container, you can optimize their environment. One way to do this is by adding feeder organisms that will help clean the environment. Some examples of feeder organisms are snails, shrimp, and cleaning fish. Find out which of these organisms is readily available in your locale.

Feed Your Fish

Once you have prepared a good home for your fish and you have added the fish into it, it's time to start feeding them. The types of food you feed your fish will depend on the type of fish you have chosen. If you have added underwater plants to the habitat of your fish, they can feed on these. Fish can also feed on insects. But if you would like your fish to grow rapidly, give them organic fish feed that is sold in stores. Fish feed can come in the form of sinking pellets, floating pellets, meal, flakes, or crumble. Feed your fish a small amount first, then observe how they react to it. If your fish gobble up the food without any issues, you can stick with the fish feed you bought. Just avoid overfeeding your fish as this isn't good for them.

Caring for fish is another challenging task, especially if you have never done it before. But it is a good challenge because you will learn a lot of things along the way. Soon, you might even be able to raise different types of fish on your farm!

Chapter 9:

What Comes Next?

Once you have established your farm, what comes next?

After learning the basics of growing fruits and vegetables along with raising animals, it's time to discuss the next steps. You will discover all these possibilities in this chapter.

Harvesting Your Produce

One of the best things about growing fresh produce in your garden is being able to harvest what you have grown. Having fresh fruits, herbs, and veggies right in your backyard means that you can just pick what you want or need simply by stepping outside. But if you want to make the most out of your crops, you should know exactly when and how to harvest.

If you grow your crops from purchased seeds, check the labels to find out when the plants should be mature. On the label, you will also find other helpful information like succession crops, seed-starting dates, and the like. Using this information, you can come up with an estimate of the perfect time to harvest. But remember that there are other factors that influence the readiness of plants including temperature, precipitation, and the fertility of the soil.

When you discover that your crops are ready to harvest, it's best to do this early in the morning. This is because fruits and veggies regain moisture overnight, which makes them juicier, crispier, and even sweeter. If you aren't able to harvest your crops in the morning, place a shade over them so that they won't lose moisture throughout the day. Also, remember that the quality of fresh produce is highest right after harvest, then it starts to decline quickly after that.

Finally, when harvesting your crops, be very gentle. If you can't pull or twist off your crops easily, use pruners, scissors, or a knife to cut them off. Doing this prevents damage to the plant, which is important because any damage could be the source of plant diseases. While harvesting, be careful with the other plants in your garden too. You don't want to end up stepping on any of them while you are harvesting. Following these simple tips will make harvesting an enjoyable experience for you. Now, let's go through some tips for how to harvest specific crops.

Harvesting Vegetables

There is nothing like enjoying a salad that's filled with veggies plucked from your garden. So if you will grow veggies in your garden, harvesting them at just the right time is of the essence.

- **Beetroot**

  If you planted your beetroots in the fall, you can harvest them before the first frost comes. If you planted your beetroots in the spring, you should harvest them before the weather turns hot. When your beetroots reach a diameter of 1 ½ to 2 inches, this is the best time to harvest them. If they grow any bigger, they might become woody. You can also harvest and eat beetroot greens.

- **Bell peppers**

  When your bell peppers grow to full size and they have a vibrant color (red, yellow, orange, or green), you can start harvesting them. Use a pair of pruners or scissors to cut the stems off while harvesting so that you don't break the branches.

- **Beans**

  When you see that the pods of your bean plants are full, bulging, and tender, you can start harvesting them. To make sure, you can pick one and split it open to check. Don't wait until the beans turn yellow. Hold the caps of the beans and break them off gently while harvesting.

- **Carrots**

  When your carrots reach a diameter of ¾ to 1 inch, you can start harvesting them. If you want to store your carrots, leave the tops on.

- **Cucumbers**

  When your cucumbers reach a length of 2 inches, you can start harvesting them. If you leave them on the plant for too long, the seeds will start hardening, the skin will turn yellow, and the flesh will taste bitter. If you plan to pickle your cucumbers, you can wait until they reach a length of 6 inches. Use pruners or a sharp knife when harvesting.

- **Garlic**

  When the summer season starts and the leaves of your garlic plants turn yellow, you can start harvesting. Use a spading fork or your hand to lift the whole plant from the soil. Do this carefully so that you don't bruise the garlic bulbs. Use a brush to brush the soil off, then place the bulbs on a drying rack until the skin turns papery and the necks dry out.

- **Microgreens**

  When you see that a pair of leaves have sprouted from the seedlings of your microgreens, they are ready for you to harvest them. You can also wait for the true leaves to sprout before harvesting. Both stages of harvesting can occur within 1 to 2 weeks after planting. Don't wait too long or your microgreens will experience stunted growth. Either that or the leaves will turn yellow. Use a pair of scissors to cut the stems of the microgreens about an inch above the soil.

- **Mushrooms**

  If you start your mushroom planting with a kit, you simply have to follow the recommended harvesting times and methods on it. But it's still a good idea to observe your mushrooms as they might be ready for picking even before the recommended times. As soon as the caps of your mushrooms turn from convex to concave, you can start harvesting them.

- **Onions**

  When you see that ¾ of the onion tops have fallen over, you can start harvesting the onions. Pull out the bulbs gently and cut off the tops. Air-dry the bulbs in a shaded place until they are completely dry before storing.

- **Peas**

  Pick the pea pods when they feel full and firm. You can pick one, split the pod open, and taste for sweetness. Just make sure to consume right away after harvesting as the quality tends to decline quickly.

- **Potatoes**

  When you see that the main vines of your potato plant have withered away, you can start harvesting your potatoes. Use a spading fork to dig them up, then place them in the sun for the soil to dry up. This will make it easier for you to brush the dirt off before storing them. Just don't leave the potatoes out for too long.

- **Radishes**

  Radish plants grow rapidly so you can harvest them between 3 to 4 weeks after planting the seeds. You should check your plants often between these times to avoid over maturity. For red radishes, harvest them when they have a diameter of 1 inch.

For white radishes, harvest them when they have a diameter of ¾ inch.

- **Salad leaves**

  There are different types of salad leaves and harvesting varies. For Swiss chard, you can continue harvesting until the plant flowers. For lettuce, you can harvest the whole head. For kale and collards, you can cut off the whole plant when they are either fully grown or only half-grown. If you want to extend the harvest, break the leaves off instead of the entire plant. For spinach, harvest the tender dark-green leaves when they are between 3 and 6 inches in length. Pick the outer leaves first and move inward. For turnip and mustard greens, you can also harvest the entire plant. Do this before the temperature drops.

- **Summer squash**

  When you see that the squash has a glossy or shiny appearance, you can start harvesting. This is the time when the squash is still tender. Usually, smaller squash are more tender than bigger ones.

- **Tomatoes**

  When you see that the tomatoes are firm and ripe, you can start harvesting them. Make sure to place harvested tomatoes in a shaded area so the quality doesn't decline.

- **Zucchini**

  When you see that your zucchinis are between 7 and 8 inches in length, you can start harvesting them. Don't leave them on the vine for too long as they tend to become harder and seedier as time goes by.

Harvesting Herbs

Harvesting herbs is much simpler. Since you won't be using a lot of herbs at a time when cooking, you can simply pluck off all the leaves and stems you need. Continue doing this when your herb plants have matured.

Harvesting Fruits

Harvesting fruits usually involves doing a taste test. But there are also other ways to determine if fruits are already ripe and ready for harvesting.

- **Apples**

  If you want to check the ripeness of an apple, pick one and taste it. Check the apples on your tree often as they can shrivel up or decay easily even while still on the tree.

- **Apricots**

  You can start harvesting apricots from late July until August. You know that the fruits are ripe when they are soft and you can easily pick them from the tree. Just remember that apricots bruise easily so you should handle them carefully.

- **Blueberries**

  Wait for your blueberries to turn blue before harvesting them. You know that it's the right time when the blueberries fall off the stems without any pressure.

- **Blackberries**

  When you see that the blackberries turned from shiny to dull in color, you can start harvesting them. Pick one blackberry and taste it first if you want to be sure of its ripeness.

- **Cherries**

  Check the color of the cherries to determine if they are ripe. You can also pick one and taste it to check if it's already sweet.

- **Currants**

  This is another fruit that you should taste first before harvesting. Red currants turn bright red when they are ripe. Black currants are shiny with a blue-black color when they are ripe. For white currants, it's recommended to taste them first.

- **Dragon fruit**

  Ripe dragon fruits have a bright pink color while the wings are starting to dry out and turn brown. If it is still green, it isn't ripe yet. If you see blotches on the skin, it is already overripe. You can also press the fruit gently to determine if it's ripe. If it's soft but not mushy, you can harvest it.

- **Figs**

  Press one of the figs on your tree to check if it's ripe. If it is soft but not squishy, you can harvest it. The color of the ripe fig depends on the variety of the tree you have grown. Wear gloves while harvesting figs as the sap of the tree might cause skin irritation.

- **Goji berries**

  You can start harvesting goji berries from the month of July until October. Pluck the ripe fruits using your hand or place a net below your plant and shake the branches gently for the goji berries to fall off.

- **Gooseberries**

  When harvesting gooseberries, you should squeeze them gently to check if they are soft but firm. Gooseberries don't ripen all at once, which is why you should check before you pluck. But if you want to make gooseberry preserves, you can pick the gooseberries even if they aren't ripe yet. Wear gloves while harvesting gooseberries because the plant is thorny.

- **Grapes**

  Before plucking clusters of grapes, pluck one first and taste for sweetness. When you discover that the fruit is already ripe, use a pair of scissors to clip grape clusters from the vine.

- **Kaffir limes**

  Allow your plant to grow and flourish for about a year before harvesting the fruits and seeds. The best time to start harvesting is during the spring when the tree sprouts new leaves.

- **Kiwis**

The best time to harvest kiwis is from late October until early November. This is when the fruits become soft and get a subtly sweet taste. To harvest, hold the base of the fruit and snap the stem off. Do this gently as the fruits are very delicate.

- **Kumquat**

You know that it's time to harvest the kumquats from your tree when they turn a bright orange color. Look for fruits that are plump and firm, then use a pair of scissors to snip them off the branches of the tree.

- **Lemons**

When you see that your lemons are firm and either yellow-green or pure yellow in color, you can start harvesting them. The best time to do this is when the size of the lemons is between 2 and 3 inches. Hold the fruit in your hand and twist it off gently to harvest.

- **Melons**

For cantaloupes, you know they are ripe if you hear a hollow sound when you knock on them. You should also detect a fragrant aroma on the fruit's blossom end. You can harvest honeydews when they have a creamy white to yellowish color with a velvety-soft texture.

- **Passion fruits**

The best time to harvest passion fruits is from the end of summer until fall. Harvest plump fruits that have a deep golden color and a slight give. Overripe passion fruits have slightly wrinkled skin but these are much sweeter than the fruits that are perfectly ripe.

- **Peaches**

  If you see that your peaches have vivid golden color and are quite soft to the touch, you can start harvesting them. Simply hold the fruit in your hand and twist it off gently.

- **Pears**

  Since pears are very firm, it's quite tricky to determine if they are already ripe. The best thing you can do is pick one of the fruits and taste it. But if the fruit comes off easily from the stem, there is a high likelihood that it is already ripe.

- **Pineapples**

  One indicator of ripeness in pineapples is their yellow color. Also if the pineapple smells tangy and sweet, this is another indicator of ripeness. Finally, you can tap the fruit to check if it sounds solid instead of hollow.

- **Raspberries**

  Once you see that your raspberries have a bright, even color, try plucking one to taste. Ripe raspberries are fairly firm, plump, and have a sweet fragrance. Pick the raspberries gently as they are very delicate.

- **Strawberries**

  When you see that your strawberries have turned bright red, harvest them right away. It's not recommended to let strawberries become overripe as they will attract diseases and insects. Don't wash the strawberries if you aren't going to eat them yet.

By knowing what to look out for when harvesting fruits and vegetables, this task will become much easier for you. After harvesting, you can decide whether to consume your produce right away or store it first.

Storing and Preserving Your Harvests

When it comes to storing fruits, veggies, and herbs, you have plenty of great options. But before you store any produce, you should clean it first. While growing in your garden, fruits, herbs, and vegetables are exposed to contaminants and bacteria. Even if you didn't use pesticides or chemicals while growing your produce, it's still important to wash each piece of produce first before you eat or store it. After washing and drying off your fruits and veggies, you can store them in the following ways.

Storing Produce in a Cool, Dry Place

If you don't plan to store your fruits or veggies for a long time, you can keep them in a cool, dry place for a while. The place where you store your produce will depend on the type of produce you have harvested. Some veggies do well in cool areas (like a basement) while others will last longer in cold places (like a refrigerator). There are even some fruits that you can just place on the countertop. If you have leafy greens, it's best to wrap them with a damp paper towel, then place them in a sealed bag first to maintain their freshness.

Placing Produce in the Refrigerator

The ideal temperature of your refrigerator for storing produce is 34°F, and you should place fruits and veggies in the crisper. Some examples of produce you can store in the refrigerator are apples, eggplants, mushrooms (place them in a paper bag first), lettuce, broccoli, cucumbers, and carrots. It's also essential to place any produce that you have washed or cut up in the refrigerator as these tend to decline quickly.

Drying or Dehydrating

These processes require the removal of the fruits and veggies' water content. Drying or dehydrating fruits makes them last longer because water is essential for the survival of bacteria. When you dry veggies and fruits, this changes their taste and texture. For this, you need a dehydrator. Then you can simply place the produce in the machine and choose the appropriate settings. Then, you can store your dried fruits and veggies easily.

Canning

While the process of canning is more common in commercial settings, when you do this at home, you will most likely use mason jars and other containers made of glass. This process involves sealing fresh produce in an airtight and sterile container. For this process, you need jars, lids, rings, a funnel, seals, and a pressure canner. You also need a big pot you will use for blanching.

Fermenting

This process involves the conversion of carbohydrates into organic acids or alcohol. This happens through the introduction of some kind of dedicated starter like whey or salt to a container filled with water. This creates a brine solution. When you add fruits or vegetables to the solution, they will start fermenting. But before you add fresh produce to the solution, cut them into small pieces first. Then seal the container and make it airtight for the fermentation process to start. This process needs at least 48 hours for fruits. Veggies take a longer time because they don't contain a lot of sugar.

Freezing

This method works with all kinds of fruits and veggies to lengthen their shelf life while preserving their nutrients and taste. However, freezing tends to alter the texture of fruits and veggies. Often, people freeze produce to use for making smoothies too. When it comes to fruits, you should only freeze them when they are ripe as they will not continue ripening after freezing. The only veggies you shouldn't freeze are leafy green veggies if you plan to eat them raw.

Making Preserves and Jams

This is one method that is exclusively for fruits. If you were able to harvest plenty of fruits, especially berries, you can make fruit preserves and jams. Simply boil the fruits in water until the liquid is reduced to the consistency you prefer. While boiling, mix and mash the fruits to bring out their juices.

Oil Packing

For this method, you will soak vegetables and fruits in vegetable oil to prevent the development of bacteria. Oil packing also adds flavor to the produce. This method is ideal for olives, eggplants, tomatoes, and different types of herbs, which you place in an airtight container along with the oil.

Pickling

This process involves preserving fruits and vegetables in a vinegar solution. As with most of the other methods discussed here, you need airtight containers for this process. Since vinegar has a high acid content, you don't have to store pickled fruits and veggies in the refrigerator. One thing to note is that pickling alters the flavor of the produce. You can also use alcohol (like brandy and rum) mixed with unrefined cane sugar to pickle your fruits and veggies for a more unique flavor.

Salting

This is another simple method of storing veggies where you soak them in a container filled with water first. Then add salt to the container until you see that the salt is starting to accumulate on the vegetables. This is an indication that the water has reached its point of saturation. Then place the container in the refrigerator for at least seven days. After that, drain the liquid and cover the veggies with more salt. Place the container in a cool, dry place until the veggies have dried up.

As you can see, there are many ways to store your fruits and veggies. You can try these different methods and see which one works best for you.

How to Make Money From Your Backyard Mini Farm

While self-reliance and sustainability are wonderful goals for having a backyard mini farm, one of your goals can also be to transform your mini farm (or parts of it) into a business. Throughout this book, you have gained some knowledge about which parts of your mini farm can be used for profits. Some examples of business ideas are:

- Selling fruits, vegetables, herbs, and spices.
- Selling animal products like meat, eggs, milk, honey, and more depending on the animals that you will raise on your farm.
- Breeding and selling animals (you need to get a license for this first).

But these aren't the only ways you can make money from your small farm. Since the business side of mini farming is a whole new ball game, there are things you need to do first. These will help increase the success of your business.

Create a Business Plan

One of the first steps you must take to turn your farm into a business is to create a business plan. Being a business owner is different from being a farm owner. Therefore, you need to do a lot of research to find success. A business plan is a very useful tool that will help you determine the feasibility of your business ideas while helping you establish realistic goals. You can learn more about business plans by going online and searching for sample plans for businesses similar to the one you want to establish. Then you can download a free template online to make it easier for you to create your plan.

Think About Your Finances

Take some time to think about your funding. Although your goal in starting a business is to earn money, you will spend money first in order to establish your business. Come up with a budget for establishing your farming business, then research all of the funding options you have. If you have enough money to pay for everything you need for your business, good for you! If not, you may have to take out a loan or consider other options. If you don't want to spend a lot or take out a loan at this point, you can always start small and build up slowly from there.

Learn How to Market Your Products

Marketing is an important part of any business. It is especially important for new businesses as this is your chance to let people know that you are selling products from your farm. These days, online marketing is very effective so you should include this in your marketing plan.

After taking these steps, you can start thinking about what other products you can offer to your potential customers. To help you out, here are some cool ideas for you:

- Sell pastured duck, chicken, and turkey meat.
- Sell ducklings, chicks, and other baby animals.
- Sell free-range and pastured chicken and duck eggs.
- Sell pastured pork and grass-fed beef.
- Establish a micro-dairy where you can sell raw cow and goat milk, butter, and cheese along with other dairy products.
- Produce and sell compost to other farmers in your locale.
- Sell manure, wood, feathers, wool, and other farm byproducts.
- Start a snail farm (if you still have space on your mini farm) so that you can sell snail eggs (snail caviar), mucin (snail slime), and the snails themselves (escargot).
- Grow and sell medicinal plants.
- Offer fruit and vegetable picking activities (if you have plenty of crops).
- Create "How To" videos and post them on various social media platforms, then advertise your products at the end.

If you are creative enough, you can think of other ideas for your farming business. With each addition to your business, make sure you research everything you can about it. Also, get all of the permits you need so that you won't run into any legal issues later on.

Chapter 10:

Avoiding and Overcoming the

Challenges of Mini Farming

While working on your mini farm can be enjoyable and fulfilling, you will also have some challenging experiences at some point. Such experiences are part of the process and you shouldn't let them bring you down. In this chapter, you will learn the common mistakes that new farmers make along with the challenges you might encounter along with how to avoid and overcome them.

Common Mistakes to Avoid When Starting a Mini Farm

Being aware of these common mistakes will help you avoid them so that farming will be a more positive experience for you.

Placing Your Garden in a Hidden Location

If you discover that you aren't allowed to have a mini farm at home and you don't want to receive a penalty from your Homeowners' Association, you might be tempted to place your garden in a hidden location. Unfortunately, if the location is hidden, there is also a high chance that the growing conditions aren't favorable there. Instead of doing this, try to find out if there is any way you can have a mini farm (even just a small one) in your backyard. Usually, this would require more work—like getting permits or written approvals—but at least you won't feel anxious each time someone passes by your backyard.

Doing Too Many Things Right Away

One of the tips you learned here is to start small. This is very important. Many beginner farmers get so excited that they try to plant too many crops while simultaneously introducing animals to their farm too. While this might seem like the quicker way to establish your mini farm, you will end up getting overwhelmed after just a few weeks. Allow yourself to get used to each element of your mini farm before adding a new one. This will make farming more enjoyable and educational for you.

Planting Crops Close to One Another to Save Space

If you have a small piece of land and you want to grow different kinds of plants, don't do this by planting your crops right next to each other. Doing this won't allow your plants to grow healthily. Instead, come up with a plan for how you will arrange your crops. You can also consider space-saving gardening methods or even growing some of your crops inside the house. Remember that plants also need space to grow and flourish so you should never overcrowd them.

Adding the Wrong Amount of Water, Fertilizer, or Mulch

Watering, fertilizing, and adding mulch to your plants are all essential for their vigorous growth. But if you add too much or you don't add enough, this will do more harm than good. In the case of water, adding too much might cause root rot and other diseases, while adding too little will cause your plants to dry up. In the case of fertilizer, adding too much might mess with the natural growth of your plants while adding too little (or none at all) might cause a delay in their growth. As for mulch, adding too much will prevent sprouts from pushing through so that they can get sunlight and air. Water, fertilizer, and mulch will only benefit your plants if you use them appropriately.

Not Weeding Regularly

Weeds are very detrimental to the health of your plants because they compete for resources. Since weeds are very hardy, they usually win. If you don't weed regularly, you will see an overgrowth of weeds in your garden in no time. The worst part is, those weeds would already have strong root systems making them more difficult to remove. So make sure to check your garden regularly so that you can pull out any weeds as soon as you see them sprout.

The Most Common Challenges and How to Overcome Them

Even if you know the common mistakes to avoid while starting your farm, this doesn't mean that you won't encounter any other issues. When this happens, don't panic. If you already expect these challenges to happen, you will be ready for them. Then you can take the necessary steps to fix the issue. Here are some other challenges you may face when running your mini farm and how to deal with them.

Unfavorable Weather Conditions

Unfortunately, this is something that none of us can control, so you shouldn't allow yourself to stress over the weather. The best thing you can do is to protect your plants and animals from extreme weather. For animals, just make sure to provide them with a sturdy shelter for them to go into. As for your plants, you can cover them with frost blankets during the cold months. You can use a canvas or canopy to protect them from the heat during the hottest months of the year. If you grow plants in containers, you have the option to bring them indoors.

Your Plants Don't Get Pollinated

This usually happens to fruiting plants as they need a certain type of pollinator to pollinate them. The solution for this issue is to attract more pollinators to your garden, and you can do this by planting more flowers along with your crops. Then avoid spraying pesticides as these can kill the beneficial insects too. Instead, check your plants regularly so that you can spot and remove any pests right away.

Too Many Pests

Speaking of pests, this is another challenge you may encounter, especially if you start growing more types of plants in your garden. The problem with pests is that there are so many types, and it can be quite challenging to spot some of those types. The best thing you can do here is to find out exactly what types of pests your plants are susceptible to. This knowledge will make it easier for you to spot and get rid of those pests when you are tending to your garden.

Frequent Occurrence of Disease

If you notice that your plants keep getting infected with diseases, check each one of them. A common cause of infections is a diseased plant that hasn't been discovered yet. Once you find that plant, pull it out right away. Then try to observe if your plants still develop diseases. If they do, evaluate your gardening practices. Go back to the tips in Chapter 4 and try to determine what you're doing wrong.

Physical Issues That Prevent You From Gardening

Since gardening involves physical activity, you might encounter some physical issues while working on your mini farm. For instance, you might experience back pains, joint pains, or you might have difficulties bending over or kneeling. In such cases, try to think of ways to make gardening easier for you. Don't spend too much time tending to your plants if it causes you pain. You can also consider growing your plants in raised beds so you don't have to bend over or kneel. Coming up with ways to make gardening more comfortable for you will make this experience less stressful too.

Conclusion:

Start Your Self-Sufficient Backyard

Mini Farm Now!

There you have it. All of the fundamental information you need to know about kick-starting your homestead garden and producing all of the food you need off the grid. Throughout this book, you have learned tips, tricks, and valuable information to start planning how to establish your mini farm.

We started by discussing the benefits of mini farming along with the things you must consider before deciding to take this challenging and fulfilling journey. Understanding the benefits will motivate you, while knowing the considerations will make you more realistic when planning your mini farm. Next, we introduced the main elements of a mini farm to help you decide what you could include in your own backyard.

In the next six chapters, you discovered how to start growing plants and raising animals on your small farm. You can keep going back to these chapters as you create your plan and while you are putting your plans into action. These chapters will serve as a valuable reference for you. In the next chapter, we discussed what you can do after you have established your farm. From harvesting and storing your crops to transforming your home farm into a business, there is a lot for you to do!

Finally, we quickly discussed the common mistakes and challenges you might encounter along with how to overcome them. This is the last thing you need to learn before you can start applying all of your knowledge to the real world. You can also learn more about self-sufficiency and homesteading at https://selfreliantbooks.com.

Now that you have gained enough knowledge about mini farming, it's time to start working. Step outside and take a look at your land. It has the potential to become a sustainable farm and even a lucrative source of income. But all of this can only happen if you start applying what you have learned. So start making a plan to transform your backyard into your very own mini farm now!

References

Arbor Day Foundation. (2018, July 11). *The best low-maintenance fruit trees.* Arbor Day Blog. https://arbordayblog.org/landscapedesign/the-best-low-maintenance-fruit-trees

Balogh, A. (2020, December 1). *Small vegetable garden ideas & tips.* Garden Design. https://www.gardendesign.com/vegetables/small.html

Beck, C. (2017, November 28). *A beginner's guide to vertical farming.* Eco Warrior Princess. https://ecowarriorprincess.net/2017/11/a-beginners-guide-to-vertical-farming/

Blogger. (2014, June 24). *Backyard fish farming – Raise fish in your home pond.* Woldwide Aquaculture. http://worldwideaquaculture.com/backyard-fish-farming-raise-fish-in-your-home-pond/

Boeckmann, C. (2021a, January 13). *10 Easy vegetables to grow from seed.* Old Farmer's Almanac. https://www.almanac.com/content/10-easy-vegetables-grow-seed

Boeckmann, C. (2021b, July 2). *When to harvest vegetables and fruit for best flavor.* Old Farmer's Almanac. https://www.almanac.com/when-harvest-vegetables-and-fruit

Bonnie Plants. (2019). *9 Mistakes new gardeners make—and how to avoid them*. Bonnie Plants Canada. https://bonnieplants.com/gardening/9-mistakes-new-gardeners-make-and-how-to-avoid-them/

Boyles, M. (2020, September 25). *4 Ways to preserve fruit & vegetables at home*. Old Farmer's Almanac. https://www.almanac.com/4-ways-preserve-fruit-vegetables-home

Bradbury, K. (2010, November 4). *Growing fruit and vegetables in small spaces*. GrowVeg. https://www.growveg.com/guides/growing-fruit-and-vegetables-in-small-spaces

Buckner, H. (2019, September 1). *12 Easy ways to extend the harvest season*. Gardener's Path. https://gardenerspath.com/how-to/hacks/extend-the-harvest-season/

Chase, A. R. (2014, April 25). *10 Ways to keep your garden healthy*. Fine Gardening. https://www.finegardening.com/article/10-ways-to-keep-your-garden-healthy

Clark, J. (n.d.). *14 Fruit vines that are pretty and productive*. Tips Bulletin. https://www.tipsbulletin.com/fruit-vines/

Coldiron, R. (2019, December 20). *Backyard livestock 101: A guide to the most common animals for urban farming*. Martha Stewart. https://www.marthastewart.com/2226271/backyard-farm-animals-101

Cowan, S. (2021, August 31). *7 Ways to extend the growing season*. Eartheasy Guides & Articles. https://learn.eartheasy.com/articles/7-ways-to-extend-the-growing-season/

Cox, M. (2017, September 6). *7 Ways to preserve your summer fruits and veggies for winter.* ZING Blog by Quicken Loans. https://www.quickenloans.com/blog/7-ways-preserve-summer-fruits-veggies-winter

Crawford, K. (2021, January 25). *25+ Best backyard grill ideas - Outdoor BBQ area designs for 2021.* Farm Food Family. https://farmfoodfamily.com/backyard-grill-ideas/

Cross, E. (2014, April 10). *Start your own simple, super-productive backyard farm.* Mother Earth Living. https://www.motherearthliving.com/gardening/backyard-farm-zmfz15mfzhou/

Davis, J. (2018, November 7). *What is backyard farming.* Try Backyard Farming. https://www.trybackyardfarming.com/what-is-backyard-farming/

Diana. (2021, May 17). *The best farm animals to raise for beginners.* Simple Homestead Living. https://www.wanderinghoofranch.com/best-farm-animals-for-beginners/

Dizon, A. (2019, August 1). *20 Most profitable small farm ideas in 2019.* Fit Small Business. https://fitsmallbusiness.com/profitable-small-farm-ideas/

Dyer, M. H. (n.d.). *Small farming tips and ideas – how to start a small farm.* Gardening Know How. https://www.gardeningknowhow.com/garden-how-to/info/how-to-start-a-small-farm.htm

Elsner, D. (2018, February 1). *Considerations for growing backyard small fruit.* MSU Extension.

https://www.canr.msu.cdu/rcsources/considerations_for_gro
wing_backyard_small_fruit

Farmhacker. (2021, January 1). *105+ Ways to make money farming a small farm in 2021*. https://farmhacker.com/make-money-farming-small-farm/

Flack, K. (2016, April 5). *Growing pains: 5 Challenges facing urban agriculture (and how to overcome them)*. Seed Stock. http://seedstock.com/2016/04/05/growing-pains-5-challenges-facing-urban-agriculture-and-how-to-overcome-them/

Forney, J. M. (n.d.). *14 Top fruit trees for home gardens*. HGTV. https://www.hgtv.com/outdoors/flowers-and-plants/fruit/15-top-fruit-trees-for-home-gardens-pictures

Freight Farms. (2019, August 12). *Top 5 benefits of urban farming*. https://www.freightfarms.com/blog/urban-farming-benefits

Garman, J. (2019, February 1). *How to start beekeeping in your backyard*. Backyard Beekeeping. https://backyardbeekeeping.iamcountryside.com/beekeeping-101/how-to-start-a-honey-bee-farm/

Gaskill, L. (2016, April 3). *Remake your backyard into a mini farm*. Houzz. https://www.houzz.com/magazine/remake-your-backyard-into-a-mini-farm-stsetivw-vs~63740706

Gemeš, N. (2020, November 15). *11 Best solar stoves (2021 Review) buyer's guide*. Green Citizen. https://greencitizen.com/solar-stove/

Glen, C. (2015, June 25). *Culinary herbs are easy to grow*. Chatham County Center. https://chatham.ces.ncsu.edu/2015/05/herbs-are-easy/

Hansen, J. (n.d.). *The easiest fruits and vegetables to grow for beginners.* GardenTech. https://www.gardentech.com/blog/gardening-and-healthy-living/8-easy-to-grow-fruits-and-veggies

Hayes, B. (2021, June 10). *12 Easiest fruits to grow in a home garden.* Gardening Channel. https://www.gardeningchannel.com/easiest-fruits-grow-home-garden/

Healthline Editorial Team. (2017, September 14). *Storing fruits and vegetables.* Healthline. https://www.healthline.com/health/food-safety-fruits-vegetables

HGTV. (n.d.). *Maintaining a vegetable garden.* https://www.hgtv.com/outdoors/gardens/planting-and-maintenance/maintaining-a-vegetable-garden

Hobby Farms. (2016, August 4). *15 Livestock breeds small-scale farmers can raise.* https://www.hobbyfarms.com/15-livestock-breeds-small-scale-farmers-can-raise

Horton, A. (2021, April 28). *20 Easiest fruits anyone can grow {beginner friendly ideas}.* DIY & Crafts. https://www.diyncrafts.com/116316/home/gardening/20-easiest-fruits-anyone-can-grow-beginner-friendly-ideas

Hosta, H. (2020, June 11). *Growing food at home in small spaces - 8 Top tips.* Eco Home. https://www.ecohome.net/guides/2228/grow-food-at-home-7-tips-for-growing-food-in-small-spaces/

Iannotti, M. (2020, October 27). *9 Best fruit plants to grow in your garden.* The Spruce. https://www.thespruce.com/the-best-fruit-to-grow-4134299

Iannotti, M. (2021, June 29). *You can have a vegetable garden even if you don't have much space.* The Spruce. https://www.thespruce.com/vegetable-gardening-in-small-spaces-1403451

Janet. (2014, November 25). *How to start a backyard farm.* One Acre Farm. https://ouroneacrefarm.com/2014/11/25/start-backyard-farm/

Johnson, C. (2021, September 9). *7 Ways to preserve your garden harvest.* Earth911. https://earth911.com/home-garden/forever-food-7-ways-to-preserve-your-garden-harvest/

Krane, J. (2018, July 11). *10 Fast-growing fruits for a speedy harvest.* Better Homes & Gardens. https://www.bhg.com/gardening/vegetable/fruit/fast-growing-fruit/?slide=slide_6bca21ed-83eb-4c77-b7cf-ceade586a09d#slide_6bca21ed-83eb-4c77-b7cf-ceade586a09d

Krantz, P. (2016, May 19). *Organic pest control solutions.* Better Homes & Gardens. https://www.bhg.com/gardening/pests/animal/how-to-control-garden-pests/

LaLiberte, K. (2021, September 28). *Control garden pests & diseases using natural habitat.* Gardeners Supply. https://www.gardeners.com/how-to/managing-garden-pests-diseases/5064.html

Landau, C. (2019, June 18). *How to start a farm, your complete guide to success.* Bplans Blog. https://articles.bplans.com/how-to-start-a-farm-and-how-to-start-farming/

LaVolpe, N. (2021, August 27). *15 Tips on how to store and preserve your garden harvest.* Old Farmers' Almanac. https://www.farmersalmanac.com/how-to-store-preserve-fruits-vegetables-garden-124627

Markham, B. L. (2016, April 14). *Mother Earth living.* Mother Earth Living. https://www.motherearthliving.com/gardening/backyard-farm-zmfz16mjzolc

Martin, K. (2021, February 12). *12 Climbing fruit plants.* Urban Garden Gal. https://www.urbangardengal.com/climbing-fruit-plants/

Masabni, J. (n.d.). *Harvesting & handling vegetables from a garden.* Texas A&M AgriLife Extension Service. https://agrilifeextension.tamu.edu/library/gardening/harvesting-handling-vegetables-garden/

Masabni, J. G. (n.d.). *10 Steps to vegetable garden success.* Texas A&M AgriLife Extension Service. https://agrilifeextension.tamu.edu/library/gardening/10-steps-to-vegetable-garden-success/

Mayer, A. (2017, July 17). *How some small farmers are raising livestock with the environment in mind.* KCUR 89.3. https://www.kcur.org/agriculture/2017-07-17/how-some-small-farmers-are-raising-livestock-with-the-environment-in-mind

Mccune, K. (n.d.). *4 Low maintenance farm animals (Have a life and animals!).* Family Farm Livestock. https://familyfarmlivestock.com/4-low-maintenance-farm-animals-have-a-life-and-animals/

McLaughlin, C. (2009, December 19). *The advantages of growing backyard produce.* Fine Gardening. https://www.finegardening.com/article/the-advantages-of-growing-backyard-produce

Mitchell, A. (2021, February 2). *8 Fruit trees you can grow right on your porch.* Good Housekeeping. https://www.goodhousekeeping.com/home/gardening/a2070 6778/fruit-trees/

Morn, S. (2012, August 6). *10 Beginning gardener mistakes to avoid.* Hobby Farms. https://www.hobbyfarms.com/10-beginning-gardener-mistakes-to-avoid-2/

MorningChores Staff. (2016, March 5). *8 Easiest vegetables to grow even if you don't know anything about gardening.* MorningChores. https://morningchores.com/easiest-vegetables-to-grow/

Mossy Oak. (2019, July 2). *Backyard farming: Creating a small, sustainable microfarm for your family.* https://www.mossyoak.com/our-obsession/blogs/how-to/backyard-farming-creating-a-small-sustainable-microfarm-for-your-family

Normandeau, S. (2021, March 25). *6 Spices you'll be amazed you can grow yourself.* Farmers' Almanac. https://www.farmersalmanac.com/grow-spices-31922

Norris, M. K. (2015, April 1). *5 Tips to raising livestock for food.* https://melissaknorris.com/tips-to-raising-livestock/

Our Backyard Farm. (2020, January 9). *Sustainable backyard farm - 5 Tips to start one.* https://ourbackyardfarm.com/sustainable-backyard-farm/

Poindexter, J. (2016, October 26). *Backyard fish farming: How to raise fish for food or profit at home.* MorningChores. https://morningchores.com/fish-farming/

Poindexter, J. (2018, March 23). *26 Tips to protect your garden against bugs, critters, and disease.* Morning Chores. https://morningchores.com/protect-your-garden/

pri02. (2019, August 24). *Everything you need to know about backyard farming.* The Permaculture Research Institute. https://www.permaculturenews.org/2019/08/24/everything-you-need-to-know-about-backyard-farming/

Qureshi, A. (2020, February 24). *Introducing green elements into backyard farming.* Blue and Green Tomorrow. https://blueandgreentomorrow.com/environment/introducing-green-elements-into-backyard-farming/

Ranch & Farm Properties. (2018, January 24). *50 Ways to make your land a profitable commodity.* https://www.ranchandfarmproperties.com/blog/50-ways-to-make-your-land-a-profitable-commodity

Robles, K. ((n.d.). *Here's why you need to get a wood burning stove.* Farming My Backyard. https://farmingmybackyard.com/warming-up-to-wood-heat/

Rural Only. (n.d.). *8 Easy animals to raise for new farmers.* https://www.ruralonly.com/blog/farm-animals/

Sanderson, S. (n.d.). *Top 10 Easy to grow vegetable plants.* Thompson & Morgan. https://www.thompson-morgan.com/top-10-easy-to-grow-vegetables

Sayner, A. (2019, March 17). *21 Of the best small scale farming ideas.* GroCycle. https://grocycle.com/small-scale-farming-ideas/

Sloan, M., & Navabpour, K. (2015, May 28). *Beekeeping basics: How to raise honeybees in your backyard.* Sunset Magazine. https://www.sunset.com/garden/backyard-projects/beekeeper

St. Dennis, M. (2017, April 18). *10 Top garden challenges and what to do about them.* Life Is Just Ducky. https://www.lifeisjustducky.com/garden-challenges/

Tanner, C. (2020, April 10). *Harvesting vegetables.* Home & Garden Information Center. https://hgic.clemson.edu/factsheet/harvesting-vegetables/

The Editors. (2021, March 7). *Beekeeping 101: Should you raise honey bees?* Old Farmer's Almanac. https://www.almanac.com/beekeeping-101-why-raise-honeybees

The Old Farmer's Almanac. (2021, August 18). *10 Ways to extend your growing season.* https://www.almanac.com/video/10-ways-extend-your-growing-season

Thomas, J. (2020, April 10). *10 Common gardening mistakes to avoid and how to fix them.* Homesteading Family. https://homesteadingfamily.com/10-common-gardening-mistakes-to-avoid/

Utah State University. (n.d.). *Harvest and storage of vegetables and fruits.* https://extension.usu.edu/yardandgarden/research/harvest-and-storage-of-vegetables-and-fruits

Vale, R. (2017, February 10). 10 Reasons to start backyard gardens in homes and schools. *Green and Healthy Homes.*

https://richmondvale.org/en/blog/10-reasons-to-start-backyard-gardens-in-homes-and-schools

Vanheems, B. (2018, August 31). *6 Ways to extend your harvests.* GrowVeg. https://www.growveg.com/guides/6-ways-to-extend-your-harvests/

Vanheems, B. (2020, April 2). *6 Quick and easy crops to grow now.* GrowVeg. https://www.growveg.com/guides/6-quick-and-easy-crops-to-grow-now/

Vanorio, A. (2020, March 21). *My DIY off-grid outdoor kitchen with brick oven and grill.* Fox Run Environmental Education Center. https://www.foxrunenvironmentaleducationcenter.org/alternative-energy-blog/2020/3/20/my-diy-outdoor-kitchen-with-brick-oven-and-grill

Wallin, C. (2019, December 19). *Ten most profitable herbs to grow.* Profitable Plants. https://www.profitableplants.com/ten-most-profitable-herbs-to-grow/

Walliser, J. (2016, December 20). *Preventing pests in your garden: 5 Strategies for success.* Savvy Gardening. https://savvygardening.com/preventing-pests-in-your-garden/

Ward, L. (2016, January 18). *How to start an urban beehive.* Hobby Farms. https://www.hobbyfarms.com/how-to-start-an-urban-beehive/

Weaver, S. (2009, February 18). *How to keep livestock and make money.* Hobby Farms. https://www.hobbyfarms.com/how-to-keep-livestock-and-make-money-3/

Welp Magazine. (2020, September 5). *Common problems for small farmers (and how to overcome them).* https://welpmagazine.com/common-problems-for-small-farmers-and-how-to-overcome-them/

Whitman, A. (2021, April 9). *Best herbs for growing indoors.* Gardeners Supply. https://www.gardeners.com/how-to/herbs-indoors/8920.html

Wickison, M. (2021, August 29). *27 Ways to make money from your small farm.* ToughNickel. https://toughnickel.com/self-employment/small-farms

Worst, R. (2020, October 9). *Backyard farming for everyone: Get started easily today!* Worst Room. https://worstroom.com/backyard-farming/

Young, M. (2018, April 9). *11 Top garden challenges & solutions to overcome them.* Farm Fit Living. https://farmfitliving.com/top-garden-challenges/

Image References/Sources

Ackermann, B. (2020). *Beekeeping.* Unsplash. [Image]. https://unsplash.com/photos/9CuGKLZQ0AU

Brown, R. (2016). *Physical Work.* Pixabay. [Image]. https://pixabay.com/photos/gardening-plant-garden-nature-1645815/

Bühne, K. (2018). *Raising Animals.* Pexels. [Image]. https://www.pexels.com/photo/photo-of-chicken-1562389/

Chung, Z. (2020). *Starting a Mini Farm*. Pexels. [Image]. https://www.pexels.com/photo/people-harvesting-apples-5528986/

congerdesign. (2016). *What Makes a Mini Farm*. Pixabay. [Image]. https://pixabay.com/photos/white-cabbage-garden-2521700/

CSU-Extension. (2017). *Drying or Dehydrating*. Pixabay. [Image]. https://pixabay.com/photos/mason-jars-dehydrated-fruit-oranges-2742757/

Ehlers, M. (2018). *Type of Animals*. Pexels. [Image]. https://www.pexels.com/photo/selective-focus-photo-of-flock-of-ducklings-perching-on-gray-concrete-pavement-1300355/

Gamstaetter, T. (2016). *Carrots*. Unsplash. [Image]. https://unsplash.com/photos/IFGVE61AAno

Hong, B. (2018). *Harvest Regularly*. Unsplash. [Image]. https://unsplash.com/photos/xEPMg4qfjOs

Khrapova, M. (2017). *Apple Trees*. Unsplash. [Image]. https://unsplash.com/photos/GbY8Xg5iTOA

Kittle, B. (2019). *Grow Plants Inside Your Home*. Unsplash. [Image]. https://unsplash.com/photos/fOZ9dh8qpVw

lumix2004. (2016). *Conclusion*. Pixabay. [Image]. https://pixabay.com/photos/apples-orchard-apple-trees-1873078/

Pinet, J. (2020). *Attract Pollinators*. Unsplash. [Image]. https://unsplash.com/photos/PVtGddsWAyY

Pixabay. (2016). *Preserves and Jams.* Pexels. [Image]. https://www.pexels.com/photo/clear-glass-mason-jars-48817/

Pontes, V. (2018). *Cows.* Pexels. [Image]. https://www.pexels.com/photo/herd-of-brown-calf-953966/

Santos, L. (2017). *Grapes.* Pexels. [Image]. https://www.pexels.com/photo/several-bunch-of-grapes-760281/

Shevtsova, D. (2020). *Introduction.* Pexels. [Image]. https://www.pexels.com/photo/green-vegetables-in-a-bowl-4117548/

Shimizu, K. (2018). *Type of Fish.* Unsplash. [Image]. https://unsplash.com/photos/SjcrpttvjiE

Spiske, M. (2018). *Container Gardening.* Unsplash. [Image]. https://unsplash.com/photos/4PG6wLlVag4

StockSnap. (2017). *Rabbits.* Pixabay. [Image]. https://pixabay.com/photos/rabbit-pet-animal-flowers-outside-2562684/

Made in United States
North Haven, CT
30 August 2023

40942767R00085